GET ON YOUR KNEE REPLACEMENTS AND PRAY!

GET ON YOUR KNEE REPLACEMENTS AND PRAY!

If You're Not Dead, You're Not Done

*Kathie Kandel Poe, Karen Kandel Kizlin,
Kris Kandel Schwambach, Linda Kandel Mason*

Nashville New York

FaithWords
Hachette Book Group
1290 Avenue of the Americas, New York, NY 10104
faithwords.com
twitter.com/faithwords

First Edition: April 2019

FaithWords is a division of Hachette Book Group, Inc. The FaithWords name and logo are trademarks of Hachette Book Group, Inc.

The publisher is not responsible for websites (or their content) that are not owned by the publisher.

The Hachette Speakers Bureau provides a wide range of authors for speaking events. To find out more, go to www.hachettespeakersbureau.com or call (866) 376-6591.

Scriptures taken from the Holy Bible, New International Version®, NIV®. Copyright © 1973, 1978, 1984, 2011 by Biblica, Inc™. Used by permission of Zondervan. All rights reserved worldwide. www.zondervan.com. The "NIV" and "New International Version" are trademarks registered in the United States Patent and Trademark Office by Biblica, Inc™.

Library of Congress Cataloging in Publication Data has been applied for.

ISBN: 978-1-5460-1019-7 (paper over board), 978-1-5460-1020-3 (ebook)

Printed in the United States of America

LSC-C

10 9 8 7 6 5 4 3 2 1

"Soli Deo gloria." *In Latin it means, "Glory to God alone."* *We recognize that God has called us to this stage for this season of our lives. It is to Him and Him alone that we give credit, honor, and praise. We sometimes shake our heads in disbelief at the doors He has opened. We go to our knees in gratitude for the doors He has opened.* *This book is dedicated to Him.* Soli Deo gloria... *Glory to God alone.*

Contents

Contents

Four Sisters,
One Voice

There are four of us writing this book, and it's pretty obvious when we're together that we are sisters. We look quite a bit alike. We like the same things. Our voices sound alike; we often move alike; we even sometimes laugh alike.

Three of us four sisters were born as a group. Kris entered the world first, followed by Karen six minutes later, and twenty minutes after that Kathie made her appearance. We three were wombmates who then became roommates. Yep, as triplets we started out as a herd and then increased. Linda was born four years later, so she is younger. She loves to emphasize the younger part.

We can finish each other's sentences and often respond in unison. We definitely have a herd mentality. It appears that we have some type of internal radar. We can't help it. We think alike.

For example: We all love purses. Kathie lives a hundred miles from where we other sisters live. She went shopping and bought a new handbag. The next time Kathie came to visit, two of the same purses were sitting on the table. Karen and Kris had bought the exact same one! It was orange. Linda didn't need to buy that one. She already owns four orange purses.

Yes, we think alike.

Three of us started singing almost before we could talk. There was a good reason for that. When we sang, people gave us money. At family reunions, church picnics, and potlucks, we were asked to sing. Pennies, nickels, and dimes followed. We liked money. Our dad thought it was a good idea to make Linda the accompanist to our childhood singing group. People thought it was adorable that these sisters were bold enough to be in front of an audience and perform. Because we were singers, we practiced together and traveled together. As we got older we did more concerts, bigger performances. It meant more being together.

We all attended the same elementary and high school and all graduated from the same university with teaching degrees. We have over one hundred years of combined teaching experience.

After college each of us married: Kris to Dave,

a pastor; Karen to John, a sales rep; Kathie married but was divorced after twenty-eight years; and Linda to Roger, a mental health counselor for school and a marriage and family counselor for church.

We all have children and currently the combined count of grandchildren is twenty-one.

Most important, we all love Jesus. We know that He is our Sustainer, Healer, Redeemer, Savior, King of Kings, and Lord of Lords.

We are all Bible teachers at our own churches. We speak together at Christian gatherings, women's events, senior adult ministries, youth meetings, and schools.

Kris has taught every age group at church, has held the role of children's director and women's ministry leader, and has been involved in mission teams and on numerous mission trips. She has written Bible studies and curriculum as well as devotionals.

Karen has led women's Bible studies, has been a women's ministry leader, and has written Bible studies and devotionals. She has served on both mission and prayer teams.

Linda has worked in prayer ministry, written puppet scripts, and worked with children's productions. She has written a prayer curriculum for her church, worked with incarcerated youth, and taught Bible studies for children and adults.

Kathie has taught Bible classes for all ages, sung on worship teams, written scripts for children's programs as well as devotionals, and she has worked in singles' ministry.

About five years ago we began sharing our faith through the written word. When we started to write books, we found our voices very naturally morphed into a single "I" and it was almost impossible to tell in our narrative where one sister's voice began and another's ended. Did we already say the four of us sometimes say exactly the same words at the same time? Yes, we really are a lot alike.

As you read our words in this book, imagine us all speaking in unison—or at least, all at once. The "I" could be Kris, Karen, Kathie, or Linda. You guess who. Often, rereading our words, we honestly can't remember who said what. We hope you won't be confused. But if you *are* confused, well, as four sisters, we're used to confusing people!

CHAPTER 1

Aging:
Drum Roll, Please!

What comes to mind when you think about getting old?

- Knee or hip replacements?
- Wrinkles?
- Wrinkle cream?
- Healthy eating?
- Eating whatever I want?
- Wisdom?
- Forgetting more than I thought I knew?
- Going under the knife in order to go out without skin flapping in the wind?
- The golden years, or silver sneakers, or the funeral preplanning appointment?

Do you remember the "talk" sometime around fifth grade when they divided up the boys and the girls? A few giggles and then an uncomfortable hush came over the room. We listened with wide eyes and gaping jaws as the nurse filled us in on stuff. It started something like this: "Now, as you get older, your body is going to change..." and it was off to the races with facts and information that made lots of us want to run for the hills.

But does anyone prepare us for the changes that take place as we get much older? Who's supposed to be doing that talk?

Bodies begin to spread out.
Hair begins to thin out.
Muscles begin to wimp out.
Feet begin to flatten out.
Eyes begin to wear out.
Teeth begin to fall out.

And maybe all of that makes us want to run for the hills. So what comes to mind when you think about getting old?

Here's my problem: When I think "old," I "think" old. And I don't like it! So I have determined not to get old. Nope, not doing it. My body may scream out for antiaging products, but my brain is still thinking youth and vitality. When I hear the word "old," I promise you—I ignore it. I don't want to get a tightly curled perm. I don't like desserts encased in gelatin...but I will always like fondue parties. Fruit Stripe gum did change my life.

Got it? I am who I am. I will not be defined by age, just like I am not going to be defined by my abilities, disabilities, talents, looks, finances. I have a mission.

This is not the curtain going down or even the curtain call. Drum roll, please. It is actually when the big music can start. Do you hear it?

There's a job to do that is just waiting for you. Every day you live, there will be a "to do" list waiting on God's table. You will never be done until the moment He says, "It's finished. You're done. It's time to come home."

Don't plan to be done until you are done, and then hopefully, you will hear, "Well done!"

Let this book be your antiaging product. It is supposed to be the face in the mirror of your heart that refuses to quit because of a date on a calendar. It is the cheerleader telling you to keep going, keep serving, keep praying. You don't have to be able to leap tall buildings in a single bound, because you have gained the wisdom to know where the front door is and have earned an access key.

Walk with us on the wild side of life on the

other side of the hill. Not *over* the hill. You heard that wrong. We're going on an adventure that will lead us to some of the lives of men and women in Scripture who refused to take "No!" for an answer. They just kept going.

> Lord God, I may have seen the top of the hill, but I want to do whatever it takes to accomplish all that You have for me. Give me energy, strength, and stamina.

CHAPTER 2

That Foreign Country
Called Retirement

Think back to the feeling you had when you finally got the job you wanted. It was amazing to know that you landed it. You were raring to go. It was thrilling to realize that within a few days you would be walking through the metaphorical doors of your career.

Then in that career there were days that were win, win, win, but there were also some that were lose, lose, lose.

Hopefully most days carried the wins.

My career was teaching.

I almost always thought that teaching was great fun, watching the light bulb go on inside a student. It was rewarding when kids got a concept or shared insight into something they had researched on their own.

There were moments that brought me so

much joy. But there were parts of the job that I really didn't like. While field trips were educational, they fell on the low end of the love-to-teach spectrum. Anyone who has tried to outlaw prayer in school never took kids on a field trip.

Usually our students were well behaved, but taking them off-site meant uncertainty and un-predictability coupled with more responsibility. One year, the other sixth-grade teacher and I took classes to a train museum. Trains are historic; without them the United States couldn't have become what it is. The museum excursion offered a train ride, along with pizza and a drink. We hoped this would be a fun time for the students, yet instructional. The ride to and from the train was an hour each way; we'd then spend some time in the museum, and the train ride itself was an hour. Yes, an easy one-day trip.

When we arrived at the museum, train whistles were available for purchase. The field trip money parents had given the kids was burning holes in their pockets. Imagine, for a moment, sixty kids with train whistles. Did I mention my dislike of field trips?

We boarded the train and traveled down the track for about thirty minutes, savoring the pizza and relishing the ride. The second half of the trip was the return to the station. The expectation in most forms of transportation is a forward motion. That expectation was wrong. Instead of making a turn, the train started backing up. Where was that tidbit of information in the pamphlet when we planned the trip? It felt like a reverse roller coaster ride. Our sixty pizza-eating, soft drink–guzzling, whistle-blowing sixth graders were shimmied, swayed, shaken, and stirred. Many of their faces took on a greenish pallor. Another bit of information that was not in the pamphlet was that the train had no restrooms.

Field trips, however educational, were not fun.

When we finally returned to the train museum station, our bus driver was frantic, fearing we would not make it back to school in time for dismissal. She wanted to leave immediately, allowing no time to let the kids walk off the nausea they felt and get some fresh air. We boarded the bus to head back. I kept telling myself we could make it, although I knew school buses weren't a smooth form of transportation, especially when kids are already sick.

Field trips can make learning contagious, but throwing up is also contagious. If one kid does it, a whole lot of others join in.

I liked teaching, but field trips made me think about retirement.

No career is easy, but when people ask, "And what is it that you do?" you have an answer. "I am a ____," and you fill in the blank. But then, sooner than you think, a day comes along where you face walking out of those doors, probably never to return. Most people call it retirement. It's daunting.

When I first started seriously thinking about leaving my career, I went to the retirement website. I clicked on the picture of a confused-looking man. He represented a link to find a retirement seminar in my local area. I had heard changes were coming down the pike for retirees in the state. I knew I needed that information, but thinking about retirement was terrifying. With trembling hands, I filled out the page, put my finger on the button, held my breath, prayed, and pressed Send. I was registered.

I sat in the seminar sweating and almost hyperventilating. I had a good job and I liked it—field trips aside. Why was I thinking about retirement? I had been at the same school for twenty-five years. I loved the people. I loved the kids. Why was I thinking about retirement? I made a living wage. I could pay my bills with some left at the end of each month. I could afford to buy Christmas presents for my kids and seven little darling grandkids. If I wanted new shoes, I could buy them. Why was I thinking about retirement? Could I cut my income and still buy Christmas presents for my grandkids? Overwhelmed, I sat listening to an expert provide, in what sounded like a foreign language, information about going to what seemed like a foreign country called Retirement. I attended a bunch of seminars. The same expert from the teacher retirement program led each of them. He saw me so often I needed to add him to my Christmas list, but I was afraid I wouldn't have the money to buy him a gift.

Retirement can be scary. Retirement is a big deal. If you've already done it, you understand. If you're facing it, you can identify with the concern over the unknown.

There are defining moments in our lives. Choosing to retire is one of those.

Why was I considering it? Other teachers had worked longer than I had. I still had a few more good years in me. No one was walking me out the door yet. I had no desire to just sit with my feet up all day or to become an expert on daytime TV.

The answer?

I believed God was calling me to a second run, a different career, a new direction. I knew there was a plan for the days after my final day as a teacher.

God made each of us for a purpose, and that doesn't stop the day we leave a career. What it means is that He has something else for us to do.

I had put in the time. I had worked enough years to retire. I wasn't throwing caution completely to the wind. God knows I need stability in my life, but it was still challenging to agree to a cut in income. It was taxing to think about. I had to process it. I had to crunch numbers. I had to play out the what-ifs. It took me a year and a half until I sent in the forms to my school corporation. What I found out is that God was okay with that. He made me cautious and a planner. He built in me the desire to know where every penny goes and how far I can stretch it. And facing retirement stretched me.

But there comes a time when, just like the apostle Peter, we have to get out of our comfortable boats and take a step of faith. I chose to get out of my boat and put my eyes on Jesus.

Lord, I'm going to trust You. I know that my income has never been my source—You are. I believe You are calling me to step out in faith and do something new and different even at my retirement age. And I am asking You to help me with the challenges. I love when I read in Your Word that when Peter took his eyes off You and began to sink, You immediately reached out Your hand and caught him. Thank You for catching me every time I begin to sink.

CHAPTER 3

Re-tire

I was driving and had about thirty miles left until I got to my house. The car was an older model with faded paint and some dents and dings, but it still had some miles left in it. It ran pretty well. I wasn't expecting any difficulties.

Then I heard a noise. I felt confident that it was something from outside the car, since I had never heard that particular noise before. I made the logical choice: I ignored it. I told myself the sound was because of the rough road, and kept driving. The noise continued. The car wasn't driving the way it was supposed to. I was having trouble steering it. I didn't want to stop. I tried to keep driving, but finally I had to pull over.

When I got out to look, I was appalled. The tire was not punctured or merely flat. There had been an eruption and pieces of the shredded rubber lay in a path behind my car. I could see the metal rim of the driver's side front tire, and there was very little tire left. It was bad—very bad. Ignoring the noise had not been the best choice. In order to get home, that car absolutely had to have a new tire.

An older model car that needs a new tire is actually a good picture of retirement. We can be like the car. Maybe our paint has faded some. We have a few dents and dings, but we still have miles left in us. All we need are new tires.

That's what retiring is. It's re-tiring—getting new tires so we can keep on going.

What do those new tires look like?

Perhaps, because we're an older model and have those dents and dings, there might be several areas that need changing. One could be a hairstyle upgrade. It was for me. One day I took a hard look at myself and thought I needed something different. My old hairstyle needed to be retired. I leafed through magazines and came up with one I thought would work. I went to church a few days after the remodel. I actually didn't think it was that much of a change, but evidently some people did.

A lady approached me. "I see you have your hair fixed differently."

"Yes," I replied, basking in the glow of the upcoming compliment. "It was time."

She said, "Oh, I'm so glad. We've been praying about that."

Wait, what? Praying about my hairstyle? PRAYING ABOUT MY HAIRSTYLE!

Hunger affects millions around the world. People are being persecuted in lots of nations. There are wars and rumors of wars. Missionaries need prayer support to spread the gospel. Yet she had been praying about my hair. And who was she referring to when she said "we"? Was it on the prayer list? Did the congregation get a confidential call asking for prayer? Was the request marked URGENT? I know God said He was concerned about every hair on my head. I guess He answered the prayer for that lady and the rest of the illusive "we" she was referring to.

Sometimes re-tire may mean an upgrade, but sometimes it may mean a downgrade. Re-tiring could involve addressing the spare tire around the middle. Again, it was for me. One of my weaknesses is food. I like to eat. I like a good steak or cheesecake or steak followed by a good cheesecake. I like food and I know this love for food sometimes leads to overeating.

Because my waist has begun to spread out, I decided I needed to go on a diet. I want to try to be the best I can be, and if that means shedding a few pounds, then so be it.

Is it fun? Is it easy?

Um, NO! The word "die" is in "diet" for a reason.

There are lots of diet programs. The ads get you with words like "delicious food," "hunger squelching," "craving killer," "sugar crushing," "easy to follow," "pounds melt away," "gut busting." Who knew it could be so easy? Okay, well, maybe not the gut-busting part, but it made me think that shedding the pounds would be as effortless as a walk in the park. I should have known, because at my age a walk in the park isn't that easy.

So I tried it. I bought one of the programs. In order to get the best deal, I had to sign up for a couple of months. I signed up for the bargain-basement, basic, no-frills plan. It was kind of exciting when the first month's food came. I opened the delivery that had been left at my door. It was one box. I'm going to say that again. ALL the food for one month came in ONE box...not a very big box. That should have been a clue as to how this was going to go.

Karen and I decided to scale the weight-loss mountain together, and because we both signed up, it saved each of us another small chunk of change. It was about enough for some candy bars—I mean a head of cabbage.

The good thing was we could eat all the non-starchy vegetables we wanted. Spinach for breakfast, broccoli for lunch, cauliflower or stir-fried vegetables, of course with no oil, for supper—it was a lot of green.

We lost weight. We both did. Maybe it was the fact that our hard-earned cash had gone to pay for this puppy, so we were sticking to it like glue. Maybe it was because it really has been tested and tried and millions of people just like me have lost weight on it. Maybe it was because limited calories really do lead to weight loss. The pounds actually melted—well, not exactly melted away, but it was worth the money. So very limited food choices and mountains of nonstarchy green paid off.

Victory!

Losing weight and a new hairdo are both great, but there is way more to re-tiring than a new hairstyle or a reduced size. Every day of our lives is to be about the mission of serving the Lord. Lots of us retire in our sixties. What are we going to do for the next couple of decades?

The new tires after retirement might look like extra time that we now have to volunteer at church, a food pantry, or a homeless shelter. Perhaps new tires resemble joining the prayer team to spend a portion of the day praying. Maybe it's writing cards and letters to shut-ins whose high point in the day is the mail delivery. A new tire could mean asking the pastor if he needs help with hospital visitation, church yard work, or painting a classroom. It could possibly look like becoming a Bible teacher since we now have more time for in-depth study of God's Word.

What areas of expertise do we have that could be shared in a different venue? What experiences or mountains of learning have we stored up that could be passed on? There is great value in what we have lived, so how can we impart that treasure? Consultant? Coach? Mentor?

Could that new tire resemble even yet another career? Are you retired or thinking about it, and if so, do you need to re-tire? What does God want you to put on so you can keep on going?

Why not ask?

The goal is to do whatever it takes—dieting, praying, serving, giving, and even a new hairdo—to be everything God wants us to be.

And speaking of the hairstyle, I guess it was a winner. Still got it! But if we meet and you take one look and think, "Nah, she needs an upgrade!" feel free to pray about it.

Heavenly Father, Scripture says not to lean on my own understanding but to acknowledge You in all my ways. I want Your path to be the path for me. Help me to take the steps You want me to take.

CHAPTER 4

Preparation "H"

We used to talk about dates and cars and clothes and football and dates and homework and dates. But here we are now with "Preparation 'H'" as the title of our chapter.

There was a time when I didn't even know what PREPARATION H® was, and I sure wouldn't have written something about it. I didn't walk down that aisle much at the grocery, but sometimes today I find myself not only visiting but lingering, reading labels. It's a sad day. It's a sad, sad day when you realize that your grocery list has more to do with getting you relief than getting you food. Antacids, stuff to help crepey skin, age spots, lines and wrinkles—I'll stop. The list is very long.

So back to PREPARATION H®. Yes, I know what it is, but I'm going to broaden its meaning a little and give you a couple of *h*'s that we should have in preparation. We need to be prepared to help people be prepared for heaven.

Packing for me is an adventure, especially when I'm traveling on an international flight. I want the most in the least amount of luggage space possible and that includes room for souvenirs on the way home. That was my plan for the tour that my husband and I were leading to Israel. When I was done packing, I had everything in two fairly small bags. I packed the same way for my husband, Dave.

I learned a long time ago that my pastor husband's heart is to be available to help anyone, anytime, anyway, anywhere. He wants to be there in an emergency or crisis, so he thinks about being prepared in case of a problem. We arrived at the airport and what had he added? Get this...

a huge roll of neon-yellow duct tape
zip ties
needle-nose pliers

I don't know how you would view those items, but they don't spell "tourist" to me.

The scout side of Dave had perfectly legitimate reasons. Duct tape is the fix-it product of all time. Suitcases tear or fall apart— neon-yellow duct tape to the rescue. Right?

Zip ties? Put name tags on the luggage, and of course you need the pliers to pull those through. It all made perfect sense . . . to him.

"Are you kidding?"

Security was more than a little curious about all of that, and then he set off the alarm as he walked through the scanners. They pulled him aside and asked him if he'd be more comfortable for the search to be done in another room. Dave said, "No." He was fine. But then they asked him to start to remove his clothes. When they got down to his undershirt, Dave began to re-think his decision of not going into a separate room. He started sweating, not because he was afraid of what they would find, but because he was afraid of how many clothes he was going to be asked to remove.

Now let me say this about Dave. He has never been a bodybuilder. He doesn't bench-press any more weight than a triple deluxe cheeseburger. There's more cake than kale about him. Finally, they realized his hip replacements were setting off the alarm, and they let him pass into the gate area.

When we arrived in Jerusalem, Dave found a street vendor selling hats.

Okay, so we could get a few hats that said, "Jerusalem." Those would be nice souvenirs for our grandsons.

He bought one hundred.

We don't have one hundred grandsons.

Why? Just like duct tape, needle-nose pliers, and zip ties, you never know when you will need them. My husband sees all of life as an opportunity to help. He wanted to be prepared to bless people. But do you know what he is most prepared to do? He's always ready to share the gospel.

He took the one hundred caps to the bus. The bus driver opened the door for him to deposit those hats, but it also looked like an open door for Dave to share about having a relationship with the Lord. He began to tell our driver about Jesus, who then prayed to receive Christ.

Okay, Dave carries zip ties, duct tape, and pliers on international flights. He buys stuff I don't think we need, but more than anything, he tells people about Jesus so they can know they are on their way to heaven. He wants people prepared to go to heaven.

Somehow, I think he has the right idea.

Dave was prepared to share his faith—after all, he is a pastor, but maybe we're not pastors or evangelists. Perhaps we feel totally unprepared for the task of sharing our faith and spreading the gospel.

Not everyone in the Bible was fully prepared either.

Shepherds were not the upper echelon of society. Their work with animals left them dirty and smelly. They weren't the guys you would invite to a stylish party, and they weren't the go-to people to spread really incredible news. Shepherds at this time had a reputation more as thieves and were not considered reliable witnesses in a court of law. So they didn't see this assignment coming. They had never in a gazillion years expected to be the ones chosen for an angelic revelation and certainly wouldn't have thought they would be evangelists. They were totally unprepared. But their lack of preparation for this event didn't stop its coming, because God did choose them. He handpicked shepherds to hear the most exciting news ever spoken, about the most incredible gift ever given. Suddenly an angel showed up to deliver the news: "Today in the town of David a Savior has been born to you; he is the Messiah, the Lord. This will be a sign to you: You will find a baby wrapped in cloths and lying in a manger" (Luke 2:11–12). God had sent His Son to the tiny town called Bethlehem. He was born in a place without even a bed. Jesus was wrapped in strips of cloth but then placed in a manger. Suddenly more and more and more angels showed up, giving great praises to God.

It was unforeseen, unexpected, and totally unbelievable. The angel told the shepherds to go and find Jesus. These guys could become witnesses to this great gift. They didn't let their lack of preparation keep them from going. They believed and hurried off to see. And when those shepherds saw Jesus, the Savior of the world, that encounter changed their lives. Their own unworthiness didn't stop them from becoming the least likely first eyewitnesses of the greatest moment in all of human history. God's preparation met their lack of preparation. God's worthiness made them worthy.

God called the shepherds to go and see, and they left to tell. It is the same for us. God calls all of us to tell the amazing gospel message. His preparation meets our lack. His worthiness makes us worthy. And He gives us the joyful task of helping to prepare others by sharing God's great gift.

Ah, yes, Preparation "h" is for helping people prepare for heaven.

Thank You, Jesus, for helping me to be prepared for heaven by coming into my life. Please make me sensitive, aware, and courageous to actively share my faith with others.

CHAPTER 5

Dawn in
the Sunset Years

Packing the car to leave with an hour-and-a-half trip ahead of us, we were anxious to be home, unpacked, and in our own beds. It was late, and we were exhausted. The sun had already set, so traveling in the dark made the trip feel even longer.

Finally we reached the driveway and the garage door opened. We were home. We had been traveling with extended family, but now it was just the four of us—or at least that's what we thought.

Dave opened the back door of the van and was greeted by a carsick stowaway. It jumped out of the car and scared the daylights out of him. A one-eyed cat had hidden himself in the back and thrown up all over the contents of our packing.

He didn't stick around to apologize. We scared him as badly as he scared us. He only left his vomit calling card and then he was on his way. It was not a defining moment, but it was a moment to remember.

Defining moments don't come every day. We expect defining moments when we're younger. We look forward to those life-altering choices. Our future is not yet set. In our younger years we lived in the world of making life-changing decisions—the career, spouse, children. In our middle years came decisions that were also life changing. Maybe the job had an opening in another state, or maybe a whole new career opportunity came along. Perhaps helping our kids realize their hopes and dreams took us into a world that we never thought possible.

And then the defining moment called retirement hits.

That may make us feel like most of the life-altering choices have passed. So when defining moments come at our age, they sneak up on us like a cat slinking around our legs or jumping out of the back of our car and startling the daylights out of us!

Moses was whiling away his hours watching sheep sleep. Day after day, for forty long years, he experienced the thrill-a-minute task of keeping his flocks safe and fed. (Sound like the job you're getting ready to retire from?) He probably assumed that the life-altering choice he had made forty years previously had set his path permanently. Then, at the ripe old age of eighty, a "suddenly" happened. He didn't see it coming. God had a plan, a big, humongous, life-changing plan for this octogenarian, and it scared the daylights out of him.

Zechariah and Elizabeth were old too. They thought they were in their sunset years. The reality was this was the dawn of a new day. God had a future in mind for their old lives that would rock their worlds and usher in His great plan. And it scared Zechariah. An angel showed up and told him he was going to be a dad. His reaction? "How can I be sure of this?"

God called Joshua to lead the Hebrew nation into battle when he was way past retirement age. God actually told Joshua he was old. When the Ancient of Days tells you you're old, you're old! But the Lord reminded him over and over to be strong and courageous.

Find comfort in the fact that Bible heroes were startled and then gripped with fear at their new assignments.

What is God calling you to accomplish during the latter days of your life? What is God using to sweetly scare the daylights out of you? What is a defining moment that you can embrace with the hesitancy of Moses, the uncertainty of Zechariah, the vigor of Joshua and leave a mark that no one else will be able to make?

I know, Jesus, that You experienced the greatest change when You willingly left the magnificence of heaven and came to sinful earth. You understand when I walk into new things. It feels scary. Please, Lord, strengthen my faith to fully rely on You in life's uncertainties.

CHAPTER 6

Get on
Your Knee Replacements
and Pray

I'm not going into this aging business without a fight, so I go to the gym. I take classes.

Actually, I didn't start at the gym. I first bought a treadmill. A one-time expense, and I would have the gym at my toe tips. It looked small in the gigantic showroom, but that thing was way bigger when we got it home. It bloomed where it was planted. A friend stopped by and asked, "Why do you have the starship *Enterprise* in your living room?" No décor in the world complements a starship.

If the *Enterprise* was going to hover in my living room, at least I was going to use it. I walked six or seven miles a day. I used it for three weeks. And then it broke. We had it repaired. It broke again. We had it repaired again. Finally after numerous repairs by different repairmen,

I called the manufacturer of the now much-stripped-down *Enterprise* and asked, "When do we declare that this is a lemon?"

My starship went to a galaxy far, far away. I joined the gym—a much better choice for me and for my living room.

I walked into my first weight lifting class and after one look at me, the instructor gently said, "Don't use any weights—just lift the bar."

The bar weighs a teeny-tiny 4.4 pounds. "Wait a minute," I thought. "I'm no weakling. I've carried groceries. I can lift ten-pound bags of potatoes in a single bound, and with a baby on my hip."

By the end of that class, every muscle was screaming at me. I ached for the next four days. One hour of lifting four wee pounds required four days of medicated ointment. But I soldiered on. I've tried aerobic classes to strengthen my stamina and core classes to slim down my middle. I even went to a boxing class.

My youngest daughter had tried it and talked me into this workout. "Mom, it'll be fun!"

"No, I really don't think boxing is for someone my age."

"Mom, anybody can take this class. There are no age restrictions, and it's a really good workout. You'll love it."

A second daughter decided to try it too. "Mom, this will be fun!"

It required no skill. I qualified. There was no special equipment needed. There were no age restrictions. I thought, "I'm not going into this aging business without a fight, so maybe a boxing lesson or two would be smart." I walked in and was, by far, the oldest person in the room filled with millennials. What fun to try something totally out of my comfort zone with a herd of twenty- and thirtysomethings looking on.

Rocky Balboa, the instructor, was encouraging. "No skill needed," he said, and reached into a box and pulled out bands of cloth to wrap my hands. I had seen this in movies. I never thought it would be me. I soon realized that boxers don't wear rings. I should have left the diamond at home; it kept digging into my hand.

The first six minutes were jumping rope. I had jumped a lot of rope in my youth, so six solid minutes of rope jumping? No problem! Yes, problem! They say muscle has memory. My muscles forgot. Then instantly I knew—it was the dumb rope; it kept catching on my feet. I tried a larger one. It was still the rope. I inched toward the back of the pack, not wanting to distract the other boxers by my skill.

Finally, the six minutes were up, and it was

time to get into our gloves. I slipped my hands inside the boxing gloves so graciously provided by the gym. No special equipment needed.

The gloves oozed sweat left by the boxer before me, or maybe a hundred previous boxers. Wet, slimy, squishy, and ripe. I swallowed to keep my gag reflex in check.

My daughter announced that her hands smelled like feet. She had definitely not mentioned foot odor with her "Mom, you'll love it!" pep talk. And she had never mentioned sweat-soaked boxing gloves.

It was time to step into the ring. Boxers glide between the ropes; I slithered under the bottom one and crawled up into the ring.

Time to box the trainer. His job was to be the punching bag. He donned safety padding and we began. I was determined to float like a butterfly and sting like a bee. I had never struck a human being in the stomach before. Oh, wait—maybe one of my siblings when I was a kid, but I didn't consider them human. I really didn't want to hurt this guy, but he told me to feel free to punch as hard as I could because he was protected, wearing his safety gear. So I did. I struck. I jabbed. I floated with the poise of a buttered fly and stung with the force of a de-winged bee. The instructor held back a snicker. I warmed myself with the knowledge that I would get him the next time, because I wouldn't wear my rings.

Finally, we were instructed to move to the punching bag. The fect smell moved with me. Boxing a bag means your hands are right in front of your nose. I lost my mental edge because I could only think about how soon I would be able to disinfect my hands.

After an hour, class ended. I had proudly contributed my sweat to the other sweat. I was totally exhausted. My daughter had not lied. It was a really good workout. I decided to go back but came home with a gift request for my husband. He didn't see this one coming. Over the years I've hinted at gift ideas for him to bless me with, but this one he had never suspected. He knows that as we age, our tastes change, our desires and wishes fluctuate, but when I told him I wanted a pair of boxing gloves, my husband's face revealed that he wondered if he had committed some major faux pas. So even though no equipment is necessary for the class, I hope my husband soon surprises me with boxing gloves.

Now, I recognize I will never be a professional boxer, and there are many things like that in my life. I don't have the skill to paint a beautiful masterpiece. I'm a terrible administrator. I fail miserably when it comes to technology. I will never play an instrument, scale Mount Everest, or swim the English Channel. There are lots of I can'ts and nevers in my life, some because I don't have the talent, some because I never learned the skill, and some that I am now too old to attempt.

But there is one area that needs no skill or equipment, and none of us will ever be too old for this endeavor. And yet, it is the biggest, greatest, most powerful thing any of us can do.

It's prayer.

Prayer is the one job, the one privilege, the one act we can do in the Kingdom that will never end as long as we have breath.

Retired does not mean done. It means we have more time. It means we can devote more energy to Kingdom stuff like prayer.

We sisters have determined that we will meet to pray. We drive around the city. We pray for churches, colleges, high schools, elementary and middle schools. We pray for the mayor, the police, the lawyers, and we pray for homes and families. We seek God for our state officials and national leaders. We pray coverings over our pastors and staff at our various churches. We've also been praying for those of you who are reading this book. We may never see your faces, but we go to the One who does.

We pray. We pray based on Ruth 1:6—that people will hear that God is at work, that He has come to the aid of His people. We seek God for revival. We knock on His door for salvation for people around the world.

And God answers.

A school in our city is known for its discord and dissension. We decided to drive around it twice a week and pray for peace to reign in that building. Not long after we started praying, a mentor walked in and said, "Is it just me, or does the school feel unusually peaceful?"

Linda started praying for a cousin to come to know Christ. He lived five hundred miles away. She prayed over and over again for any Christian neighbor to invite this cousin and his wife to a Bible-believing church we knew in that city. She asked the Lord specifically for them to hear the gospel and respond by accepting Christ. Later she went home for a family reunion. The cousin was there and saw her coming and ran right toward her. "Linda, I want you to know that I have become a Christian." She was stunned and asked how it happened. "I was invited by a neighbor to go to his church where my wife and I heard the gospel and we accepted Christ." He used the exact words Linda had prayed. It was the very church she had mentioned in her prayers.

I'm not going into this aging business without a fight, but I am really not going into eternity without the fight that is waged on my knees or in a wheelchair or from my bed. I can drop to my knees, even if those knees have been replaced.

I'm going to seek God for the world, my nation, my state, my city. I pray for family, churches, friends, schools, and kids. I cover people I don't know, and who won't realize until eternity that God was answering prayer. I can seek God when I rise and when I lie down again at night. I can pray anywhere, anytime, at any age, and in whatever state I am in.

God moves when we pray. Prayer packs a punch, and it has such a powerful fragrance.

We can be older than dirt, too old to do some of the youthful things we once did. Our eyes can dim with age, but our prayer influence will never dim. Our stance may be a bit shaky, but His stance will never shake. Our abilities may diminish; God's never will.

Here's the blow-by-blow: Put on the gloves. Get on your knees. Fight one more round. No skill necessary.

Dear Lord, You are the One I want to be present and active in every area of my life. Help me every day to get in the ring and fight one more round in prayer.

CHAPTER 7

Leave Your Pride
at the Door

Here's something that every single one of us walking through that door marked SENIOR has in common. We all used to be young. Our bodies used to work when we asked them to. If we said, "Jump," our limbs asked, "How high?" Today, we give the command and the muscles smirk and tell us, "Sorry, don't you remember? We went into retirement." As youngsters, if we ate ice cream, our bodies whispered, "Thank you," and turned it into energy. If we eat ice cream today, our bodies say, "Yum," and immediately turn it into fat.

We are united by the downward spiral of aging bodies. We can stave it off a bit, but it will eventually get all of us. Youth fades. Old age happens. But we don't live with just physical transformations; we experience emotional challenges too. Eventually we move from the front seat in life to the back. We aren't the ones recognized—our kids are. It's a rude, but inevitable, awakening. We learn that God is not done raising us. Life lessons remain to be learned from the back seat. We have opportunities to grow even when we are no longer in the limelight.

It was the opportunity of a lifetime when Kathie's daughter, Faith, was invited to be in the cast of a movie based on the life of Esther. Faith was told she could invite one other young woman and two others to also participate in the film. My daughter, Lindy, was the young. Kris and I qualified as the others. The four of us traveled seven hundred miles to enjoy the spotlight of the big screen. We were super excited. Our dalliance into the world of movie stardom would be something to tell the grandchildren.

We arrived. No, we didn't qualify for a dressing room or trailer on the lot. We slapped on name tags and were directed to the movie set, where the author of the screenplay greeted us with these words: "Leave your pride at the door."

What did that mean? Was this like a coat check? Did we get a receipt? Seriously, what did that even mean?

This was a big-time movie—bright lights, gorgeous wardrobe, famous actors and actresses. Standing behind the author were the director, producer, assistants, makeup artists, and wardrobe people. They read name tags and whispered. Faith's and Lindy's names were whispered; Kris's and Karen's were not.

Our first stop was makeup. This would be soooo fun—getting our makeup done by a real Hollywood artist. It would be an absolutely fabulous opportunity to see how makeup should be applied to our somewhat aging faces. We could take home the techniques to erase wrinkles, enhance cheekbones, and bring out our natural maturing beauty.

Kris sat in the chair. The makeup gal was impressed with her fair skin and gave the compliment every woman wants to hear. "When I'm YOUR age, I hope I look this good." Then the lovely twentysomething makeup artist said Kris and I needed no makeup. Our faces would be splashed on the big screen with NO MAKEUP!

My youthful and already beautiful daughter, Lindy, and young and gorgeous niece, Faith, were given blush, lip gloss, mascara—the whole enchilada. But for Kris and me? Nada. I wear makeup. I actually do need makeup. I wear it to the grocery. I sometimes even wear it to the gym.

The makeup I wear has changed over the years. When I first started wearing cosmetics, I purchased makeup that added a youthful glow. A little blush, a bit of mascara was all I needed. But then, as I got older, I bought the stuff that said enhancing, then erasing, finally age defying. When I went to my grandmother's funeral, someone told me they had never seen her look more beautiful. I wondered what kind of makeup the undertaker had used.

I felt a bit of panic when I heard "No makeup." This was the big screen. Not even light makeup or even natural-looking makeup. Zero—none! We were not in a position to argue. This face was going to be naked on the big screen. "Leave your pride..."

The makeup artist did tell us we needed to get our skin sprayed a darker, more Middle Eastern shade. We slinked off to the tanning room deflated but suddenly hopeful that maybe our soon-to-be sun-kissed skin would look like we were once again youthful. Lindy, Faith, and I were handed sheets with which to cover up. Kris was given a hand towel. She just stared. Good thing it was all women; that hand towel wasn't going to cover much.

They sprayed our faces, arms, legs, and feet. Lindy and Faith were blessed at birth with lovely olive-toned skin. The girls turned a gorgeous shade of bronze. Kris and I didn't emerge sun kissed, but rather bright orange—the color of Sunkist, the soda. We were so glad we came! No makeup, bright orange skin, and on the big screen. "Leave your pride..."

We went to the hairstylist. We clung to the fact that at least we would have pretty hairstyles. Lindy and Faith took their turns in the chairs. The stylists were pros and their work on the girls was lovely. They rose from the chairs looking every bit the part of a candidate for queen.

Then it was my turn in the chair. The stylist took one look at me and pinned my hair flat against my head. She pulled out a can of black hairspray and sprayed my hair jet-black. Kris's was parted down the middle, combed straight, sprayed black, and finally tied with a scarf that forced her eyebrows too close to her eyes. We were a study in black and orange, perfect for Halloween. As quick as that, we were ready. My stage name could have been Skullcap. And Kris? She resembled Jabba the Hutt. We began to pray that no one we knew, ever had known, or ever would know would ever come to this movie.

On to wardrobe, and it was here that the sheep and goats really were separated. Lindy and Faith were escorted into the chamber with pageant-ready, silken, satin, rainbow-colored, jewel-encrusted gowns.

Kris and I were herded into a corner where the costumes were large beige-and-orange gunnysacks. All these floor-length garments were exactly the same burlap bag with arm slits—that is, except the one given to Kris. Hers took ugly to a whole new level, because it was embellished with a massive flounce that swished back and forth and polished the floor with every step she took. Dressed in burlap, no makeup, horrible hairstyles, orange skin, we were ready for our big-screen debut. "Leave your pride..."

Lindy's and Faith's names were called. "Do you have any people with you?" they were asked.

"PEOPLE?"

I had pushed through twenty-four hours of hard labor to bring Lindy into this world. I AM NOT HER PEOPLE! But it turned out that my training as a mom had well prepared me for my role in the movie. I was cast as Lindy's servant. And let's face it—sometimes as moms we feel that way. She sat on a pillow. I sat at her feet. She ate grapes. I handed them to her.

This was not what I expected when I agreed to

be in a movie. It was not glamorous or exciting. This was flat-out humiliating. As I sat at Lindy's feet, looking horrible, feeling worse, and handing her grapes, I questioned why I had come.

Then God whispered.

Being in this movie meant doing what the director and makeup and wardrobe people said. No arguing, no discussion about how I looked or felt or what I expected. They knew what they wanted. I simply had to follow. And yet, how often had I argued with the Lord about a job He wanted me to do, because it didn't go exactly the way I thought it should? Would I trust that God knew what He wanted and follow Him?

God spoke loudly in that whisper.

I left my pride at the true Door, Jesus, and in humility asked Him to forgive me and make me a more obedient participant as He cast His roles. The day had truly been humbling. I had no lead part, no beautiful part, but from the back seat, I learned a valuable lesson in submission. "Leave your pride at the door." I now understood what it meant.

Graciously, God also allowed every scene Kris and I were in to end up on the cutting-room floor.

Jesus, I confess there are times that I think and act as if the world revolves around me. Help me to recognize those self-centered moments. I want to be an obedient participant in Your plan for my life.

CHAPTER 8

Ninety Is the
New Forty

I don't love going to the gym. I love walking out. The best thing about a 5:00 a.m. workout is 6:00 a.m., when it's over. I go because it's good for me to move; it improves my health, balance, and overall life. It's a good thing, but movin' ain't easy.

The instructors are perfectly toned, can do all the exercises, lift large amounts of weight, run and talk at the same time. I can barely walk and breathe at the same time. I do have a six-pack; it's just that they're all two liters. At the gym I've learned a new language. I've known for many years what high heels are and have worn them, but high knees? I now know how to clean and press—not clothes, but with a weighted bar. In every class I'm the worst. But even though it's hard and I hate it and I look pretty dumb, I go.

I went to the launch of a new class in January. Nearly two hundred people filled the room. When a new class launches, the instructors sometimes give out prizes. I like prizes. When asked who was the youngest in the class, a twelve-year-old proudly raised her hand. They called her to the front of the group. She gladly accepted her gift card and skipped back to the crowd.

My daughter looked at me.

"Why are you looking at me?"

"You know they're going to ask who the oldest person in here is."

I glared back at her. "I'm not the oldest." Surely I wasn't the oldest. I didn't want to be the oldest.

Sure enough, the question came: "Who in here is over sixty-five?" My hand slowly crept up. I looked and only one other person raised his hand. The instructor insisted we come to the front. They handed him a gift card. I like gift cards. They handed me a men's XXL Muscle Milk shirt. What does "muscle milk" even mean? And MEN'S XXL? I like gift cards. I slinked back to my spot, so glad I had come. I go to the gym because moving is good for me, even if it's hard.

But there's another kind of moving that's even harder.

My daughter's family needed a bigger house. My husband and I were thinking about downsizing. We offered to let them buy ours for a price they couldn't refuse.

Have you noticed that lots of us older folks face downsizing? Maybe you're one of the blessed ones who planned well and you can spend your golden years in the family home. But for many of us, the stairs seem a lot steeper than they used to, and the basement laundry room feels like it's so much farther away than it was a few years ago. A smaller house, a condo, moving in with the kids, an assisted-living apartment, or a senior-care facility might be on our horizon.

We were looking to find a smaller house. Our kids said yes to our offer. They simply had to sell their house first. They put it on the market and two years went by. Two years! I doubted that I would ever be moving, but God was preparing me. The day came when the phone rang and I heard, "Mom, we got an offer on the house. We're taking it." Suddenly I realized my husband and I were now homeless!

Once the offer was made, things proceeded rapidly. We looked for a house, but none of them resembled my home. Our daughter, son-in-law, and kids moved in before we moved out.

Our house hunting escalated to a fevered pitch. I was terrified I was going to regret ever thinking about moving.

Eventually we found a house. Then the "not fun" part really ramped up. Downsizing is downright tough. I had to look at everything and decide what to keep. A few of those decisions were not too hard. Old worn-out underwear and socks were, of course, throwaways. I should have done that years ago. In case you're judging me, I challenge you to check your dresser drawer.

But there were other decisions that were really hard. Gifts that came from the kids or grandkids, furniture pieces bought for just the right corner of my old house, dishes that I used for Christmas were not only things; they were memories. Yet many of them had to go. They were not going to fit.

And it wasn't just the stuff—it was the house itself. We had lived a year or two in other places and then moved, but the move to Southern Indiana was permanent. This became home. This was the place where we raised our children. Moving meant leaving the home where I put my children to bed, served many, many family dinners, and created tons of Christmas memories. I hear laughter in the walls. Stains on the carpet cause mc to remember. So, moving has been painful. I've wept a few times. I've even gone into the closet, closed the door, and wailed.

Change is hard but inevitable. Moving can be one of those "I don't like it" changes. We can get mad. We can cry, complain, or yell, but it won't change the reality of change. Sometimes the decision even gets taken out of our hands. Our kids insist for our own safety that we must move. Our health becomes too precarious for us to stay where we are.

We can make ourselves sick, angry, and bitter at the need to move, or we can get on board. I decided to embrace the move, and it's given me new freedom. I'm a little bit lighter in the possessions category. And I like the feeling. I don't have as much stuff to dust. I don't have as many dishes to wash. I have less furniture to walk around.

I have asked myself the question, "Do I really want to spend the last run of my life dusting furniture, or do I want to spend my time doing Kingdom things I'm more available to do since my children are now grown?" What I've discovered is that God's plans are big, even in a smaller home.

No doubt about it, movin' ain't easy. Because we were experiencing a major move, I wondered what it might have been like for Sarah in the book of Genesis. She and Abraham made a move from Ur along the Chaldean countryside. We don't know exactly what she experienced, but let's lift the tent flap and consider what could have been her story.

Sarah was close to retirement age, and this was home. She had lived her life in Ur. Even with the heartbreak of childlessness, she and Abraham had been happy. Maybe she was one who would never have wanted to move away from her family and friends. This is where she would spend her golden years. Sarah knew Ur. Ur was home. It was familiar. Now at her ripe old age, she could lie back on her camel-hair sofa with her feet up. Life was good; retirement would be even better.

And then…AND THEN…Abraham came home and announced, "God called and we're moving."

How could this be God's best for her life? There must be some mistake. Maybe she didn't want to downsize. She didn't want to start over. How could this be God's plan?

God said He would bless Abraham. How is this blessing? Giving up everything? Saying goodbye to all that is familiar and comfortable? Walking away from family and friends? How is this blessing? How is giving up her life what God wanted for her? How could it be what God wanted for her aging husband? Weren't they too old to start over?

God's plan for Sarah's life included way more than her comfort. It entailed a bigger assignment than just spending her days with her feet propped up. God's plans are big even in a tent.

And she would not have known in the first sixty-four years of her life that this was coming. She could not have seen this on the horizon of God's amazing plan when the call came for them to move.

God doesn't reveal the whole story all at once. He walks us down the path, and the miracle of His plan unfolds as we walk in it. In an "only God can do this" kind of miracle, God was going to renew her youth. God was going to restore her vitality. Ninety was going to become Sarah's new forty.

Was moving at her age hard? I'm sure it was. At the age of ninety, when she held her newborn son, Isaac, she would have said it was worth it.

> *Father, please make me willing to move when you say, "Move." Help me to see every change in my life as a chance to grow and as an opportunity to further Your Kingdom.*

CHAPTER 9

Too Busy
to Quit

There *are* perks to getting older. A big one is discounts. Who am I to question when a business wants to determine a certain age as being worthy of a discount? Another plus is that if I forget a name or have to hunt for my keys, I can call it a senior moment. And of course there is the fact that there are small children in my life who throw their arms around my neck and call me Grandma.

However, there are some things I don't like. I don't like the phone calls that begin with, "Hello, senior." They're annoying and interrupt my day with a recorded voice trying to get me to buy a product that I don't need or want, but the only option is to press 1 to order. I hate that my bones creak when I sit, and I hate the wrinkles that have shown up on my aging face. I'm really glad I get to wear glasses, because they're a good cover-up for the undereye bags my face has decided to embrace. I don't love that it takes twice as long to look half as good. Too often my body makes up its own mind about how it's going to look. At my age if something doesn't wear out, spread out, leak out, or fall out during the day, it's a good day.

And then, of course, there is retirement. On the one hand I love that I am no longer tied to the clock, but I don't love that it's looked on as being the end. I can leave a career but never God's calling. So I refuse to look at retiring as if I'm walking out of something, but rather that God has called me into something new. The person staring at me from the mirror is old. That might mean doors are closing and not everyone wants to hear what I have to say, but age is not a reason to stop trying. My quest is obedience—to God. Aging takes place on the outside, but it's not an excuse to stop serving God. Rather, I have decided to look at wrinkles as reflections of wisdom and character on the inside, not as a reason to quit.

There are some seniors who approach their last years with resignation—"I've worked all these years, so now I'm done." The pages of Scripture show us people who quit too early. One who comes to mind is Isaac. When Isaac lost his sight, the lights dimmed. He could no longer recognize faces. He couldn't make out the details of the landscape. That is a miserable thing. Our eyesight is precious, a gift from Almighty God, but it happens: macular degeneration, cataracts, detached retinas. It was awful that it happened to Isaac.

However, Isaac could still feel, smell, taste, hear, experience, carry on conversations, talk with God, talk about his walk with God, share with the family his life story, pray, laugh, and love. Instead, Isaac decided he was dying. He called in the older of his twin sons to make sure he gave the final blessing to Esau. "Prepare me the kind of tasty food I like and bring it to me to eat, so that I may give you my blessing before I die" (Gen. 27:4).

He focused on his next meal, not his next assignment. We can't be sure how old he was. We do know it would be decades before he died. Did he spend his last years living? Or did he spend them dying? There is little more said of him until his death. His sons buried him at the age of 180.

When we look at Isaac's desire to bless, it seems on the surface to be noble. But when we realize that Isaac still had decades to live, we see that it was a premature move.

Okay, he did have some trouble seeing. Yes, he was in the twilight of his life, but Isaac still had at least another twenty years. What great things could he have accomplished for God in that time?

Isaac hadn't just lost his sight; he lost his vision. He lost his purpose. Our lives are not to be about dying. Our lives are to be about living and helping others to live.

He told himself he was done. And because he believed it, for the last part of his life, he was done.

What about us? Have we looked so much at the end that we lose sight of the now? We can't spend more time thinking about dying than we do about living.

Should we take steps for retirement?

Sure!

Is it okay to have the funeral preplanned and prepaid so that someday the kids won't have that sad burden left on them?

Absolutely.

But what are we doing right now? What difference are we making for the Kingdom of God today?

We have this time now to make our lives count.

God will take us home when He's ready. Until then, let's not lose sight of His vision.

Dear Lord, I do not want to hold back because of ailments, pain, exhaustion, inadequacies, or age. I don't want to check off my life in years, but, Jesus, I want to live my life moment by moment for You. Please give me eyes to see what You have for me each day.

CHAPTER 10

No More
Dreams to Dream

In a high-end home furniture store I saw a desk with a remote control that raised and lowered it to any height. It could be transformed from a sitting desk to a standing desk in seconds. The salesman commented to me, "Sitting is the new smoking." A desk that provides the option to stand for a little while during the day is a whole new world. You can even purchase ones that are treadmills, so you not only stand, but you can get your steps in while you're at your computer. Walk and work. Run and work. Sweat and work.

Why?

Because the amount of sitting we do each day is growing. Many of our careers and much of our work have sitting woven into the very fabric of the day. We spend hours at our desks and then hours in our cars for the long commute home and then the remaining hours of the evening sitting in front of the TV resting, because it's been such a taxing day.

And the result? "Sitting is the new smoking." Here's the conclusion: It's bad for us to sit that much.

And then after all that sitting, we go into retirement, and is that where the sitting really begins?

So what should we be doing? Heading out the door to purchase the treadmill desk? Joining the gym? Scheduling treks up and down the stairs every hour or so? Jumping rope? Taking a boxing class so our hands smell like someone's feet? All good, but is that the sole solution?

Walking away from a career and into retirement may sound like the goal of a lifetime, but sometimes it leaves our faces in the dust of despair, and we ask ourselves why we ever thought about the golf course when we had a perfectly good job to run to every day.

Jobs offer purpose, security, prestige, power, income, parameters, and value to our lives. Retirement may not. Careers often link who we are with what we do. When we walk away from the job, we look into the mirror and might run face-to-face into someone we don't even recognize. Perhaps our lives have become so intertwined with what we do that now we don't know who we are. We retire and suddenly it feels as if there are no more dreams to dream. We aren't sitting at a desk; we are sitting on the shelf. And shelves are not that comfortable. There are no dreams there.

God never intended for us to be on the shelf or to live a life without dreams. Knowing the Lord means there are always dreams to dream, places to go. Jesus told His disciples to go. Go! Go into Jerusalem, Judea, Samaria, and then to the ends of the earth. His call is to go, not to sit. Does it mean we get on a plane destined for some foreign soil? It could. The going just might entail going across the world. Whose lives would be changed if we did? Whose hearts would be moved if we were willing? Who would thank us in eternity if we went? If God calls us to go, then why not go? Can we trust that God does know what He wants for our lives?

Yes, it could be across the world, but it could also be across the street; the ends of the earth might be our own neighborhood or our own family. It could be at our home churches. Working with middle school or high school kids could be training the next great evangelist. Inspiring college students could lead to a college revival. Mentoring adults could change lives that in turn change lives.

Physical limitations can play a role. Does that mean we have an excuse to sit? NO! Because the going may be through prayer. Even though we may be in our homes, we are going when we get on our knees in prayer and stand alongside missionaries and ministries.

The call of God has no ceiling. Age has never played an ending role. The disciples never stopped sharing. Where would we be today if they had decided to just sit?

Sitting is the new smoking, so refuse to sit! Dream dreams. Be willing to dream them with Him.

Father, sometimes it feels as if my hopes and dreams are gone, but I know You have a mission in mind for me. I don't want to be sitting on a shelf. I want to be making a difference. I commit every day of my life to You, Lord.

CHAPTER 11

The Race Is On

Candy has sure changed over the last half century. In the fifties and sixties there were choices like marshmallowy circus peanuts, tasty Turkish Taffy, tiny wax bottles filled with delicious sugary syrup, and jelly beans. Jelly beans came in about seven flavors: cherry, lime, orange, lemon, grape, licorice, and white. What was the white, anyway? I hated the licorice ones. I thought they were gross. But ooh, the red ones—they could be used as lipstick.

Today jelly beans have totally stepped up their game. They come in a plethora of flavors. Buttered popcorn, doughnut, coconut, an array of soft drinks, and different kinds of chocolates and caramels to name just a few of the truly wonderful selections of this tiny little treat.

With all those choices and only a minimal

amount of calories, you can experience a virtual buffet of desserts. That's a mouthful of fabulous.

But then...

Jelly beans take disgusting to a whole different level. Flavors that taste like spoiled milk, rotten eggs, dead fish, stinky socks, and grass clippings can find their way into bags of the beans that will eventually find their way into our mouths. Our mother had a recipe that used dandelions as the main ingredient. I have to wonder if that was the inspiration for the grass clippings flavor.

But stinky socks? Really? That's a flavor?

Let's think about that for a minute. How do the manufacturers know what stinky socks taste like? Do they take the dirty socks from their kid's hamper and run boiling water through the foulest ones to brew up a type of putrid, skunky sock tea? Can you imagine the scene in the tasting room for that?

My grandkids think the repulsive ones are hysterical, so I have to be wary if they offer me jelly beans. I'm good with buttered popcorn or coconut, but I can assure you that I have no desire to find out what funky, old gym socks taste like.

However, these little tiny jelly candies offer some other benefits besides taste. They can be used to give a jolt of energy to runners. My son-in-law carries the high-energy sports ones when he runs or does long bike rides.

My daughter called to tell me that he was going to run a marathon. She invited me to help cheer him along the way. I said yes. Marathons are over twenty-six miles long. Think about how long it takes to drive twenty-six miles, but doing that many miles on foot?

At the starting gate there were about as many different costumes for the runners as there are flavors of jelly beans. And just like jelly beans they can range from the traditional to the strange.

Some of the runners moved really fast right out of the gate, some jogged, and some walked. But every single one of them was in the race.

My son-in-law is not a professional athlete, but he knew to pace himself. He carried the sports jelly bean variety to give him a burst of much needed energy to keep him going.

He finished, not first or second or even one hundredth, but he crossed the finish line. He was exhausted, completely spent. It had taken hours of continual running to get done. There were times when he wanted to quit.

Just imagine how it feels when you get to mile marker thirteen and realize you have as many miles still in front of you as you've just finished.

At mile marker twenty your muscles rebel at the thought that more than six miles still loom ahead. They twitch, contort, spasm. Marathons are a challenge. You have to stifle the mental voice that screams at you to stop.

He didn't stop. He kept going.

Water; high-carb snacks like oranges, bananas, and jelly beans; and hearing the applause as he passed certain points all kept spurring him on. He knew we were watching. He could hear us yell his name.

Marathons are long, grueling, tough, but worth it when you cross the finish line. You have the overwhelming awareness that you did it. You didn't quit; you kept on running. The "well done" accolades carry enormous value. And hey, maybe your socks can be sold to make jelly beans.

You know, life is kind of like a marathon, and in these later years it might feel like the last few miles are becoming the toughest to run. Maybe we started out jogging, sprinting, or galloping, but we've slowed a little. Our pace isn't nearly like it was.

So let's stop here at a checkpoint. Are we still in the race? We haven't quit, have we? It's hard when we hear the inner voice that says, "You can't finish. Just quit." Don't listen to that voice even if you're moving pretty slowly. It really doesn't matter how fast you're running. What matters is that you're still in.

My mother-in-law was still in at 102. Oh, she moved pretty slowly. She kind of shuffled and could only manage that with a walker. She was old, but up until the day she died she was in the race. Her course had taken her to a nursing home. She didn't want to be there. She asked family members to please take her home. But she needed a lot of care, so she had to be in a place that offered it.

At 102 Mom still looked pretty good. Her face was fairly wrinkle-free. She was a walking commercial for the face cream she used every night. It must have worked. She was so adamant about it that she often hid the tube. At the nursing home, she was convinced that someone might come into her room at night to steal it. We tried to assure her that no one was going to, but she continually found new places to conceal it. Unfortunately she then forgot where she hid it. She'd get kind of frantic, so we'd have to hunt through drawers, dirty laundry, pockets, and sometimes we'd find it stuck deep between the cushions of the furniture.

She couldn't move very fast, but she was still moving forward, and her concern was that people would know that they were headed for heaven. She shared with staff, other residents, and doctors.

One afternoon I walked into the nursing home to visit with her. When I approached, Mom was talking to the occupational therapist. She was talking with him about the Lord.

What I didn't know was that twenty-four hours later she would take her final breath here and her first breath in heaven.

Let's back up and say that again. Twenty-four hours before she died she was talking to someone about Jesus. She didn't know they were her last few hours. She didn't know her life would be over in a short time. She didn't know that she would soon see the One she had just been sharing about.

As I reflect on Mom's life, I have to ask myself a couple of questions. What will I be doing twenty-four hours before I die? Will my passion for the Lord be evidenced? Even if my gait has slowed to a shuffle, will I still be in the race?

There was a man in the Bible by the name of Methuselah. He was Noah's grandfather and lived 969 years. If we add up the years given in the biblical account, we discover that he lived until the year of the flood. In Jewish circles there is a story that says Methuselah died seven days before the flood came on the earth. It is possible that Noah closed his grandfather's eyes in death right before he entered the ark and God closed the door.

That's important because Methuselah's very name was a prophecy. A couple of meanings include "When he is gone, then it shall come," or "His death shall bring." Every time his name was spoken for 969 years, it held a prophecy of something that was coming.

But what was coming?

It was the judgment of God. One hundred years before Methuselah's death, God spoke to Noah and told him to build an ark. Talk about a second run for Noah. The boat itself was a testimony that something really big was going to come, and every time someone called to Methuselah they were exclaiming that this big event was on the horizon.

Up until the day he died, Methuselah's life announced that something was coming and that people needed to get ready for it.

What message am I leaving for others?

Mom's message spoke loud and clear: "Know Christ as your Savior." She lived it until God took her home.

In the last few weeks of Mom's life, God gave her a great gift. Now, at first glance it didn't look like a gift. It didn't feel like a gift, and it was one Mom would have gladly returned if she could have.

The amazing thing that God gave was a bigger opportunity for her to share Christ at the age of 102 than she ever would have had if she had stayed comfortable and resting in her little room at home.

How many lives were impacted in the nursing home by her conversations about the Lord? We will not know until eternity.

She didn't want to be in the nursing home, and she could have let the hurt and disappointment turn her into a bitter senior. She didn't. She used every opportunity to talk about Jesus. She continued to serve out her mission.

The next day my daughter and I went to see her again. When we arrived, she was looking in one of her dresser drawers. I thought she was looking for her face cream. She wasn't. She said, "I need to get things together. I think I'm going home today."

She desperately wanted to go back to her home. We gently explained that she was not going to go home right then.

Little did we know.

We sang and prayed with her.

We had to leave. My grandson had qualified

to run in the state cross-country meet. He's following his dad and becoming a runner too. It was something we didn't want to miss. He was prepped, ready to race, energy beans packed. What we didn't know was that when he would be beginning his race, she would be finishing hers.

Just a little while later we received a call that she was unresponsive and being transported to the hospital. We left immediately, but then we got the message that there was no need to hurry.

She had been right. She was going home.

No question, Mom's age set her apart. But what defined her was her concern for the people she met to know for sure they were going to heaven. She was always ready to share—well, not her face cream, but about the Lord. Mom had a mission for every day of her very long life.

So do we!

Just so you know, at the funeral we tucked that tube of face cream right next to her in the casket. We didn't want her to have to hunt for it.

And just like Methuselah, up until the day Mom died, her life was announcing that people needed to be ready for eternity.

Are you in the race? Do you need a little jolt of energy or a cheerleader calling your name? Here's something that's so much better than jelly beans. We find it in Hebrews 12: "Therefore, since we are surrounded by such a great cloud of witnesses, let us throw off everything that hinders and the sin that so easily entangles. And let us run with perseverance the race marked out for us, fixing our eyes on Jesus, the pioneer and perfecter of faith" (vv. 1–2).

Keep running.

> *Father, I am in the race and am determined to fix my eyes on You. I am trusting You to be the pioneer and perfecter of my faith. Please help me not to grow weary or lose heart.*

CHAPTER 12

What's in Your
Hand?

What's in your hand?

What is it that God wants us to look at through a different lens? What do we have that could be repurposed? What things in our lives could have a second run?

Take a sewing machine, for instance. It's usually not on the top of a list for a mission donation. Most churches don't designate the Easter offering to purchase one. Not many people would view it as a ministry tool, but it is.

Jodi knows exactly how valuable it is, because it has joined her for a second run.

Oh, that sewing machine has seen quite the workout through the years. It has been used for costumes, doll clothes, even home furnishings, but no one knew what it could really do until a few years ago.

Jodi's daughter-in-law works as a child life specialist at a well-known children's hospital. Her title speaks of life, and she often has the great joy of seeing sick children begin to thrive and weak children gain strength.

But there is also heartbreak in her position. Death is sometimes the whisperer. Some of the infants simply cannot overcome their conditions. The battle is waged with all valor, but the battle sometimes becomes the valley of the shadow of death.

With tearstained faces and trembling voices, the parents of these babies sob out their good-byes and with them the hopes and dreams that accompany every parent's heart: the first giggle, those toddling steps, entering kindergarten, the touchdown that would bring home the win, the new dress for the prom, the graduation party, watching their son pick out the perfect diamond.

Hopes are defeated, dreams are crushed, and the world spins out of control. All the future choices and shared experiences are never to be.

There is no way to bring comfort to a heart that is so grief filled, but there is a way to bring one precious choice.

Jodi's daughter-in-law brought her the idea. It had spilled out of her heart as she witnessed the pain and agony in the eyes of parents who had to close the eyes of their infant children in death.

She asked Jodi to use her sewing talents to make gowns and suits for those tiny infants, the ones who had fought the good fight but simply couldn't fight any longer. These are the ones whose parents had hoped to welcome home, but these little ones had taken their final breath and were instead welcomed into their eternal home.

There would never be a wedding gown to choose. There would never be a search for the perfect tux. But the parents could choose one tiny outfit that would hold in its folds all the choices they wouldn't get to make.

This was not an original idea, but it was new to Jodi. For her it would be a whole new world opened to a ministry that she had never known.

For Jodi, it is a second run.

But it is also a second run for the gown.

It begins with a wedding gown.

Bridal dresses carry the memories of the march down the aisle, the vows spoken, the rings exchanged, and the first dance at the reception. It is a very special gown for a very special day.

But what is the shelf life of a wedding dress? It's worn for one day and then hung in a closet or folded carefully in tissue paper and placed in a box.

What if instead it could be used to become the fabric of a different memory? These wedding gowns could be refashioned to carry tiny newborns into the arms of their Heavenly Father.

The dresses are donated and the process begins. The lovely lace, the beautiful pearls, the unique adornments are carefully kept. The tiniest of patterns is chosen. She sews with the image before her of parents only ever choosing one little outfit for their child.

This one.

The elegance of this tiny outfit must carry the love, joy, and hopes this mommy and daddy had for their little one.

Jodi knows that one small garment cannot bring healing, because this is the darkest of valleys. Her task is something very small, but it is something. It is one moment for a choice in a sea of choices dashed.

But Jodi learned firsthand the beauty and impact one little gown could make.

She attended a reception for those who have joined this ministry. The keynote speaker not only shared about the ministry; she shared her story. She had walked this path herself.

Jodi listened to her describe the long flowing gown with a train that had once flowed over a petal-covered carpet. But for its second run, it swaddled the speaker's own little one. Jodi recognized the description of the gown. It was one that she had lovingly labored over at her sewing machine.

But this gown not only had the story of the sweet little angel who wore it; it held a history behind it. It was made from the wedding gown that Jodi's own daughter-in-law's mother had worn. It had been taken from a closet to be re-fashioned. The train was so long it even draped over the coffin.

Infant coffins are never pretty. This gown brought an unexpected beauty.

She knew at that moment she had made a difference.

This story is about my friend named Jodi. It is about a gown that won't ever be stored covered in tissue paper but instead covered in love. It is a story about a sewing machine. It's a story about second runs.

The question is, what's in your hand?

Dear Heavenly Father, I know You have gifted all Your children for ministry. What is it that I have as an ability, talent, or possession that can be used for Your service? Please show me where and how You want me to serve. Help me to be willing to live out my calling.

CHAPTER 13

Are You Divas?

"Are you divas?"

That was the first question out of the mouth of the literary agent who had agreed to meet with us. He didn't start with, "Tell me about your book." He didn't ask how we would bring a unique voice to our writing. He didn't ask to see a few chapters, or if we had any experience, or if we had any letters after our names, like PhD.

He didn't give us the chance to impress. He simply started with one very simple question: "Are you divas?"

Are ... we ... divas?

Petulant, peevish, spoiled, cantankerous, a trial to even be around, divas believe the world revolves around them. They bark out commands and expect to be obeyed. They are challenging to work with, difficult to please.

So that question has caused us to pause and ponder.

First of all, how important do we think we are?

How much do we strive to impress by our carefully, immaculately groomed appearance?

Now, don't get me wrong—we believe everyone should attempt to be the best that they can be. We try to hide the flaws and cover up the weaknesses and blunders.

So, how successful have we been at that?

Kris, on a cold winter's day, nearly walked out of the house with just her long underwear. Nothing says diva like leaving the house with your slacks still hanging in the closet.

At my daughter's wedding I realized too late that my husband, John, had been munching on chocolate chip cookies in the car right before the event. I didn't know till I exited the vehicle and he said, "Honey, what's all over the back of your skirt?"

"What? What do you mean 'what's all over the back of my skirt'?"

There was chocolate smeared across my cream-colored dress, and I was soon going to be walking down the aisle and mounting the stairs in front of the crowd, lighting a candle right next to the groom's perfectly groomed mother.

There wasn't a person on the planet whose first thought would be that the brown on my skirt was CHOCOLATE!

So our diva-ish appearance doesn't always make an appearance.

Did we grow up pampered and spoiled by overly indulgent parents?

We grew up in a family that wasn't dirt poor, but we lived right around the corner from dirt poor.

Our dad was a meat cutter at a grocery. Our mom stayed at home with six kids. We ate the meat and produce that were too far gone to sell. We didn't know for a long time that bananas were actually supposed to be yellow.

Every year our parents planted a huge garden, and when I say huge, I mean one not measured in feet or yards but in acres. We planted, weeded, picked off tomato worms and potato bugs, harvested the vegetables, washed, dried, and sold produce to the grocery. A lot of what we ate was the bruised or slightly rotten stuff that wouldn't sell.

But even before that bounty arrived, Mom found a gift outside that she and Dad feasted on in the spring. There was treasure in the yard. It's called dandelions.

Our parents thought it was nearly manna

from heaven—after all, it was free and showed up in the grass every morning. Mom wilted it in some type of brown vinegar-and-egg gravy. We thought it was repugnance on a plate.

And then there was cheese. Cheese in the deli section of the store gets sliced off of those perfectly round or square blocks. But before that happens, the dried ends need to be removed, and of course those couldn't be wasted. So growing up, snacks at our house consisted of a variety of cheese ends.

If it was out of date, past the code, a little bit rotten, a tiny smidgen spoiled, too dried out, really ripe, growing in the yard, or even moldy, it came to us. And the side benefit was that none of us got sick much because our daily diet came equipped with its own form of penicillin.

So maybe we're divas in the world of homemaking. Do we stun our families with our *Iron Chef America*–like talents and skills?

Linda always says that she makes a mean pot of swill. Our grandparents raised pigs. Swill is the garbage and waste from cooking, mixed with water to make food to slop the pigs.

She's tried to step up her game. Recently she cooked a delicious baked squash. Her husband, Roger, complimented her gourmet creativity because he thought she had added corn to the dish. He thought it had the right amount of crunch.

"Corn? Oh, he liked the corn...Wait a minute." Suddenly she remembered that she hadn't added corn! Linda ran to investigate. She realized that the corn had faces. IT WASN'T CORN. The squash was infested with worms. Roger had to have a mountain of chocolate to wash away the worm aftertaste.

Worm swill spells d-i-v-a every time.

Okay, so maybe you get the picture that we don't always have it all together. We do plenty of the dumb, silly, ridiculous, and downright stupid.

Divas R Us is not sending the welcoming committee for us.

But what if we did have it all together in the areas of attire or homemaking skills, or what if we were tycoons in the world of finance or had celebrity status in some way, shape, or form? Would we then be privileged to play the diva card?

Here's the answer: "NO!"

The world does not revolve around any of us. None of us, no matter how old, are here to be served; we are all called to serve.

It doesn't matter how many letters we have after our names. It doesn't matter if we own whole islands or boats and houses on every continent. Our bank accounts, our life status, our political aspirations, our names in lights do not mean that we are the big shots who get to be served.

If we run a country, run our family, or run errands, the call is still the same.

Sometimes we as seniors think our age gives us the right to bark out commands. Sorry—age doesn't come with that status.

Perhaps, because of pain or ailments, we start believing that we can treat people as less or as pawns to do our bidding.

That doesn't cut it either. We don't get a pass.

Jesus owns everything. He has the most important letters ever written after His name: King of Kings and Lord of Lords, Immanuel. He sits on the throne and rules the universe. His credentials include Creator, Sustainer, Healer, Redeemer, and Savior, to name just a few.

And yet, He set it all aside for us. He took on the very nature of a servant. He gave up everything so we could have everything. He left heaven so we could go there. He gave His life so we could have life.

We are called to take up our cross and follow Him.

The call is to serve. We are to serve when we

are young, when we are middle-aged, and with thankful hearts when God graciously allows us the longevity to reach our golden years.

Serving God and serving others is our mission.

None of us get to claim the title of diva. We all have the privilege of embracing the title of servant.

Are you a diva?

I hope the answer is a resounding, "No!"

> *Jesus, You set everything aside for me. You did not consider equality with God something to be grasped, and You took on the very nature of a servant. Thank You. I want my life to reflect that same attitude as I take up my cross and follow You.*

CHAPTER 14

When You
Hit the Wall
and See Stars

Stop and think about words for a moment. There are words that take up space in our vocabulary and can carry little to no meaning. Words such as "uh" and "like" and "just" can simply become filler words in our sentences.

But then there are power words: "gold medal," "Super Bowl," "promotion," "valedictorian," "win," "tax refund," "90 percent discount." Some are victorious, but then there are some words that are defeating. One of the most crushing is "cancer." It carries a wallop when you run into that wall. It knocks people down or even out for the count for a while. For some it takes a lot to get up off the mat.

The treatment options are varied and usually grueling.

The treatment for Debbie was radiation.

The goal was to win. It wasn't to slow, cause a temporary interruption of, or simply bench the cancer until halftime. No, cancer treatment is meant to be aggressive and thorough. It is designed to conform to the camping slogan, "Leave no trace." All of those rays targeting the cancer are meant to wipe it out once and for all.

Cancer treatments can carry huge side effects. Nausea, pain, hair loss, a gray pallor to the skin, loss of appetite, and fatigue can all join you at one time or another on your way to the cure.

Debbie was no exception.

The treatment for the day was over. She went home, retreated to her bedroom, settled beneath the sheets. There are times the cancer ordeal needs to be faced while lying down and resting.

Her husband came to check on her. His compassion was evident in his eyes. She had suffered radiation treatment. What would this mean for her? What side effects would she face?

He gently adjusted her blankets. He gasped. A bright yellow light radiated from her skin. What had they done? No one had warned them of this.

The radiation treatment had begun that day, and now her skin was glowing.

Debbie couldn't hold it together any longer.

The tears came.

But not from fear—she erupted into laughter.

She had covered her body with glow-in-the-dark star stickers.

She couldn't help it. For Debbie this was the chance of a lifetime. Nothing would be more fun than seeing her husband's face as he encountered that otherworldly glow.

Her stickers were shouting. They were picketing. They were neon signs declaring to the big gun cancer that though she might sometimes have to lie down, she was still standing on the inside.

She was down, but she wasn't down for the count—she was down for the win.

She met cancer with glow-in-the-dark stars.

In our eyes, she is a star too!

Isn't that a great story? Cancer doesn't seem like it should be involved in a good story, but this is what we have found: God wants to use everything, even the very hard things in our lives.

Every life has a story, and every story has a life, because God can take the mundane, the funny, the difficult, the sad, the shocking, and the very challenging and use it to point to Him.

The apostle Paul wrote in Philippians 1:12 that what had happened to him had really served to advance the gospel. He had been flogged, beaten, jailed, and stoned, but saw God use it all.

So what events have happened in our lives that we can use to further the gospel? They don't always come as a second job or career or opportunity to serve. Sometimes they come cloaked in something darker, only to later be seen through His light.

Here's another story:

"I am honored…"

To become Miss Universe? To receive a Golden Globe? To get that big promotion, raise, corner office with the huge windows?

Not this time.

Her exact words: "I am honored that God chose me."

For the mission field? To join a ministry staff? To give a huge donation to the church?

Not this time.

The honor? Amie was diagnosed with an astrocytoma. To put it simply, she has a malignant brain tumor.

Her story began with changes in the way her world felt. Life seemed chaotic, dark. Her normal life did not feel normal. It felt overwhelming. She wasn't on top of it. It was on top of her.

Standing at a cash register and trying to make change was an impossible task one day. She was embarrassed and upset. She couldn't do the math.

But Amie leads a busy life. She is a wife and mom and home schools and chauffeurs her kids. That kind of "go, go" life can make anyone want to check the freezer to see if that's where you left the keys.

But this was different. Life seemed different. Shadows were coloring her world and she couldn't understand why.

It was a Sunday morning. She felt great. The family was at church, but almost as soon as the service had finished, her body took over. Sharp pains shot through her arm and down her left side.

Amie was having a grand mal seizure.

An ambulance ride to the emergency room and then tests—the CAT scan was read immediately.

Her husband, Adam, is a neuroradiologist. He was in the room when the results went up on the screen. He fell to his knees. He knew what he was seeing.

How do you tell your beautiful wife that she has a softball-sized tumor? How do you explain the unexplainable?

Adam walked into her room. She could see it in his eyes. She didn't have to hear his words. They were facing the battle of a lifetime.

Their busy everyday life wasn't everyday anymore. A new journey had begun. It meant surgery.

During the operation, she slept only for the time it took to open her skull. She had to be awake during the removal of the tumor so she could answer questions. She was never afraid. Adam couldn't be in the room, but she knew Jesus was holding her hand.

The surgeon probed and asked Amie questions. "How many fingers do you see?"

"Two."

"How many this time?"

"Three."

"Okay, now how many do you see?"

"It looks like a black tunnel."

It meant he could cut no deeper.

It wasn't painful. She heard conversations, but Peace is what spoke. After five hours, a drill secured the bolts to reattach her skull. The surgery was over, but the journey was not.

"Seven to ten years."

Adam was brokenhearted as he shared the news. Amie thought surgery would mean a cure. She realized then that they were still trudging a rocky path.

At first Amie lived in the "I might nots."

"I might not be here for graduations, weddings, the grand moments in the kids' lives. But I also might not be here for the everyday, the mundane, the little moments."

Seven to ten years is heartbreaking, but Amie lives on two levels. The first is ground level, and it heard the prognosis. The second is heart level, and it sees the hand of God.

Was this a death sentence?

Perhaps, but Amie and Adam have not allowed that to be the final word. They have prayed through every round.

Sometimes a second run simply means getting up to fight another round.

And there have been rounds…rounds of radiation.

Her radiation meant a claustrophobic, "stay perfectly still" submission to the war weapons used against this type of cancer.

Trauma caused her to lose patches of hair after the surgery. More was lost from the radiation, but a very lovely side of Amie emerged.

Joy filled her eyes, her smile, her face, and her life.

Don't misunderstand; this is a fight, a raging battle. For the first year, she woke feeling as if she were punched in the stomach.

But it would not win. Fear would not move in. She wouldn't be angry with God. Heartbreaking words would not be allowed to direct her heart or mind.

Amie's life is showcasing God's answer. She

shared these words: "This has not taken God by surprise. He is always good. You can't do it without Him. When you spend time with Him, He brings the joy."

She's a little forgetful. Noise bothers her, but her message?

"I am honored that God chose me."

Miss Universe? The corner office? The ministry staff?

Not this time.

Amie has been diagnosed with a malignant brain tumor.

It is her platform. It is His message.

"I am honored…"

Her story points directly to Jesus. Every one of our stories can.

Lord, I know that nothing takes You by surprise. You are a healing God, so right now I pray for those who are battling illnesses. I know that You do not waste anything, so please help me face whatever comes into my life. Give me the grace to share You even in the deepest valleys.

CHAPTER 15

An Old Dog
Teaching an Old Dog

I have taught Bible classes, and I had a dog named Maggie.

Now, normally these two things wouldn't go hand in hand, but stay with me, because in this case they actually do.

Maggie was one of several dogs that we've owned over the years. She was the kind of dog that didn't bark. Maybe right now you're thinking about a nice, sedate, quiet little canine that would sit patiently, silently, just waiting to be called.

No, Maggie was a beagle.

Beagle puppies get you. They're so cute with their short little legs and their long little ears. They trip as they run toward you and as babies they have a pitiful, mournful little cry. It pierces your heart.

Yes, they get you, and we were got. Cute, adorable, precious Maggie came home with us. But beagle puppies grow up to be adult beagle dogs. They don't bark; they howl. From somewhere in the deep recesses of that low-to-the-ground, squatty body would come the most awful sound. Her bellowing was a lot like the tornado siren that goes off in the neighborhood. No longer was her cry pitiful and mournful. It especially wasn't little. Maggie was loud. Her voice pierced our eardrums.

The neighbors complained.

We tried to keep her from howling. Our yard was fenced to keep her contained and entertained.

Here's another thing about beagles: They love to dig. We had to go around the bottom of the fence and attach horizontal boards to keep her from digging her way out. Yeah, our yard looked lovely.

Beagles also love to jump. They especially love to jump on people. We'd walk out the back door all ready for church and Maggie would greet us with her muddy paws. So more fencing was added to our yard to keep her away from the back door. She could romp in a big space in the rest of the yard, but the area around the back door was off-limits.

Our cute little adorable puppy grew into a digging, howling, jumping dog. Of course we loved her, but she could be annoying.

As I said, I have taught Bible classes. For a while one of my jobs at church was to open the teaching time for the kids and other teachers in the main area before they were dismissed to their classes.

I could share a Bible story or lesson of my choosing. It was a great deal of freedom, but I took it seriously. I prayed and prepared days in advance so I could teach the message that I felt God wanted for that Sunday.

Most often on Mondays I would settle on the idea and then write out my lesson. Then on Tuesday and throughout the rest of the week I would tweak, refine, and practice what I was going to say.

One week, though, I really struggled. I began my prep on Monday as I always did, but I couldn't decide on anything. I got out old Sunday school lessons. Nothing. I flipped through the pages of my Bible for age-appropriate ideas. Nothing! It wasn't that I didn't find Bible stories; it was that I hadn't found what was right for that week.

On Tuesday I tried again. I asked the Lord for an idea, but I couldn't come up with anything.

Maggie was overly annoying and disturbed my brainstorming. She had dug a hole under the fence and was in the area we had made off-limits to her. Yes, there she was at the back door. Instead of studying I had to go out and board up the hole under the fence. I gritted my teeth and grabbed the hammer and nails.

By Wednesday some panic began to set in. My deadline for ideas was past due. I should have been in the reviewing and practicing stage. I prayed more. "Lord, I need help. Please give me what You want me to say." It seemed like Maggie was louder and more rambunctious than ever. I was so annoyed with her I was having trouble concentrating. It seemed like she just wanted my attention. She dug another hole, and again I heard her at the back door. How was she doing that? Ugh. More fence fixing.

On Thursday I felt like my brain was in desert mode, dry. But Maggie was in hyperenergetic mode, busy and loud.

Friday I had a headache because I had been using my brain too much and gritting my teeth too much because Maggie was such a distraction. I prayed more. "It's Friday and I have nothing. This is getting serious. I can't go to teach without an idea. Lord, You have never let me down. Please give me what You want me to share with the kids."

On Saturday I determined that I was going to study until I was done. I had fixed the fence to keep Maggie out multiple times that week. I hoped I could prepare my lesson undisturbed.

Then I heard a noise at the back door. It couldn't possibly be Maggie. I went to look.

Are you kidding me? There she was. She had again gotten into the very small area right at the back of the house. How was she doing it? Why was she doing it? I couldn't believe it. That dog couldn't do anything in that space. It was too small. She couldn't run; she couldn't chase squirrels. It was a very tiny section. There was nothing for her to do but sit, wait, and wail. I couldn't understand why she wanted to be there since she had an entire yard to play in.

Frustrated, I put her back into her part of the yard and hammered more boards into place to try to keep her away from the back door.

But then I decided to watch her. I wanted to see how she kept getting out. Honestly, that fence was patched so many times I didn't think it was possible for there to be a place for her to escape. Our yard fencing looked like something the Little Rascals had thrown together.

It didn't take long. As I watched, Maggie

found a place where a little of the wire fencing was still exposed. She wriggled and squeezed herself through it. She was crying and pulling herself through a space where she could push up into some of the sharp wires. It hurt her to do it. It was work for her to manage it.

That dog was going to unbelievable trouble, even enduring pain to get to my back door.

Why?

And then it dawned on me. Maggie just wanted to be near me. She could have played, run, jumped, chased squirrels, but that's not what she wanted. She wanted to be close to me, her master.

It was a profound moment. Maggie was willing to endure almost anything to be near me. Instead of her comfort, she made a choice to be as close to me as she could get.

Suddenly I had to ask myself a hard question. What was I willing to endure to be near my Master? What choices was I making?

That week I had asked God many times to show me what He wanted me to share. He did—I just wasn't paying attention. God used that annoying, howling, digging dog to share truth with me. Maggie was willing to endure a lot to be close to her master. I knew it was the challenge for that week for the kids, but it was also a challenge for me and the other adults I would be speaking to.

What am I willing to go through so I can spend time with my Master, Jesus?

Am I willing to give up my time to spend time with Him, praying and reading His Word?

Am I willing to face inconvenience to be with Him?

Am I willing to make Him a priority?

Or do I put off my time with the Lord and tell myself that perhaps I'll get to it tomorrow?

What's more important?

Jesus taught us about spending time with the Father. Luke 5:16 says that Jesus often withdrew to solitary places to pray. Over and over again He left the crowds so He could spend time with God. He modeled for us how important it is to spend time with the Master.

If Jesus needed time alone with God, how much more do I need that time?

When we pray, we are talking with God. When we read His word, He is speaking to us.

So, are we spending time with Him? Do we read our Bibles? Do we study so we know what His Word says? Are we talking with Him?

If the answer is no, then maybe we need to ask ourselves another question: Why not?

Almighty God, You are the Creator and the Sustainer of everything, yet You choose to have a relationship with me. I don't want anything to keep me from sitting at Your feet, my Master, my Heavenly Father.

CHAPTER 16

A Little North of Middle Age,
a Little South
of Rigor Mortis

It was cancer—one of the worst diagnoses, with the worst prognosis. The surgeon opened him up, saw the amount of cancer, and then quickly closed him back up. The cancer was everywhere...a death sentence. I was the only daughter still living close to home, on campus at college about thirty minutes from our house.

What do you say? What do you do when someone you love is staring death in the face? How do you help? Dad was starting treatments. He was still weak from the surgery but had to start chemo. There was zero time to waste.

After Dad's surgery, I went back to campus feeling helpless. I could pray, and I did. At school I had great friends. They wanted to take my mind off my dad, so they talked me into playing a basketball game. "Well, okay," I thought. "Basketball might be a good stress reliever." It turned out it was going to be a DONKEY basketball game.

If you're thinking of the video game *Donkey Kong*, you're way off. This was going to be a game played in front of a live crowd riding real, living, breathing, snorting, bucking, bladder-relieving, colon-emptying donkeys.

I called home.

"Mom, tonight I'm playing a basketball game—donkey basketball. You and Dad need a good laugh. Please come!"

Our grandmother was staying with us at the time as well. "And bring Grandma too."

"Oh, I don't know. Your dad is having his first treatment today, and I just don't know how he'll feel. We'll see."

I hung up the phone. I knew what "We'll see" meant. It almost always meant "No!"

I couldn't blame her, though. She had so much on her plate. Her dad—our grandfather—had passed away in February of that year and she had cared for him. Then just a few months after Grandpa died, Dad was diagnosed with cancer and was now starting treatments for those inoperable tumors.

But I had invited them, and so I hoped they would come. After all, I had said yes to donkey basketball, and that might be worth seeing.

That night a semitrailer truck drove up to the back of the gymnasium.

My friend Bonnie grew up on a farm. She's the good friend who had gotten me into this in the first place. I told her to make sure I got a sweet-natured animal, since I was not remotely used to farm animals.

"Okay!" was all she said. It sounded like a verbal contract to me.

The sound of the door lifting on the trailer and the wafting smell of feed, straw, animal, and excrement permeated the area.

Something I never considered when using live animals was their basic body functions. Again, I was not raised on a farm. I assumed the animals would be wearing diapers or waterproof pants or were duly trained to use the accommodations outside for their needs.

I assumed wrong. The donkeys' owner passed out shovels.

"What? Is this for what I think it's for?"

"Yes!" came the reply.

Wait—I hadn't signed up for potty patrol, but I did sign up and had given my word. I was in it for the long haul, or should I say the long shovelful haul? With shovels in hand, our team waited as the owner prepared to hand us the reins of our sweet animals.

He brought out the first donkey. "Oh, he's so cute!" I said. He looked like a stuffed animal. Honeypot was his name. He literally made you want to talk baby talk.

"I'll take Honeypot! I want Honeypot! I need Honeypot. Please give me Honeypot!" I begged.

But the owner handed the reins to my friend Bonnie. Remember, she was raised on a farm and was used to large farm animals. Honeypot was not large; he was small. Rightfully he should have been MINE! There was that verbal contract. Bonnie skipped away, delighted with her sweet-natured, long-lashed, cute, petite Honeypot.

I was next. A little of my fear had by this time subsided, having just seen Honeypot. But then I heard, "Whoa, whoa, WHOA!" from the owner.

The trailer was dark; the lights were not very good. I couldn't quite make out what my sweet-natured animal looked like. Honeypot's sister perhaps? Sweetie Pie maybe?

"You're getting Rigor Mortis!"

"Huh? What? How? WHO?"

"Rigor Mortis!"

Rigor Mortis? Wait—isn't rigor mortis what

sets in upon death? I can't have Rigor Mortis! I need Honeypot or Sweetie Pie or Cutesy Lucy or Darling Darla or whoever—*just not Rigor Mortis, the death animal!*

Besides, Bonnie and I had that verbal contract! I'm not a farm girl—Bonnie is. Give her Rigor Mortis.

But I was handed the reins of the biggest, meanest, evilest, stubbornest animal—RIGOR MORTIS. And my life as I knew it was over.

A few minutes later, we were given the donkey basketball rules:

Rule 1: Never, under any circumstances, let go of the reins!

Rule 2: You have to be on your donkey to shoot the ball.

Rule 3: Keep your shovel handy.

The whistle blew; the game started. There was Bonnie, already gleefully gliding along on Honeypot. Bonnie was a good six inches shorter than me, and her feet still dragged on the floor as Honeypot ran all over the gymnasium.

The other players were all on their donkeys, running around, doing their jobs, shooting the ball, playing the game.

And then there was Rigor Mortis. He had come into the game with his own agenda. He had determined that he was not going to work. He was done with work. He refused to get into the game. Let me reiterate: He was absolutely, unequivocally, categorically NOT going to do what he was asked to do.

And he had become quite skilled at his technique to ensure that under no circumstances was he going to get into the game or do any work or cooperate or obey what the person holding the reins wanted him to do. He bucked and he bucked and bucked and then bucked some more. I pulled on the reins, he bucked. I tried to get on him, he bucked. He bucked at the crowd and he bucked at the other players. He bucked at the other donkeys. He bucked at the sound of his own snorts.

I could feel my muscles tighten as he jerked on the reins to buck again. Suddenly it dawned on me why he was named Rigor Mortis. Every fiber of my being was stiffening while trying to get him to cooperate.

Between bucks I caught a glimpse of the people in the crowd. Shockingly, there were Mom, Dad, and Grandma. They had made it to the game and in that moment they were forgetting the woes of the world. But that's not all—

they were bent over laughing. Not just a simple giggle, but a guffaw of laughter, a cleansing, relieving, cathartic belly laugh. They were laughing so hard that Dad was stretched out, pounding the bleachers, and Grandma was sprawled out on another bleacher, laughing so much she couldn't remain upright. Mom was laughing hysterically, caught in the middle. Laughter is such good medicine.

For the entire game, I tried to manage Rigor Mortis. Several things happened:

I never let go of the reins.
I never got on Rigor Mortis.
I never got the ball.
I never made a basket.
I never let go of the shovel.
I never moved from the spot where I started,
because he refused to move from the place
where he had started.

Rigor Mortis never stopped bucking.

And I had never seen my parents and grandmother laugh so hard for so long.

"Thank You, Lord, for Rigor Mortis!" I prayed.

Sometimes when life hands you Rigor Mortis,

there is a bigger plan, a bigger picture, a bigger work taking place.

I can also say that I was glad it was the weekend. When it was over, I went home and rested—I actually collapsed...I think rigor mortis had begun to set in.

Laughter had released some of the deathly shadow that was hanging over our home. It was a good night for my parents and grandmother, albeit not so good for my aching body, but I was okay with the death donkey, even though I never actually got to ride him.

And that stubborn, unmovable creature has taught me a valuable lesson.

Rigor Mortis refused to move. He had reached a point in life where he had determined that under no circumstances was he going to move from where he decided he was comfortable. Maybe he had reached the stage in life where he was a little north of middle age. What age that is for a donkey, I don't know, but maybe he had reached a point where he felt like he had earned his rest.

What is amazing is that his refusal to work, with all his kicks and bucks, actually took way more energy than getting in the game. He missed the fun of the moment, the applause of the crowd, the "good job" verbal rewards and the pats on the back from his rider. He wore himself out refusing. He was a donkey-basketball donkey and he missed his purpose because he refused to get in the game.

I'm a little north of middle age, but I'm still south of rigor mortis. I still have some life in me. I don't want to miss my purpose.

Rigor Mortis, the death donkey, missed getting in the game. What about you?

> *Oh, Lord, I want to move to get in the game, but sometimes I'm weighed down with the things of this world. Please let nothing keep me from doing what You have called me to do.*

CHAPTER 17

Alone

Alone!

At the age of fifty I became single. I had never been single before, and when I say I had *never* been single before, I mean it. The fact that three of us four sisters were born part of a group means we were not even alone in the womb. I grew up with a team around me and we made decisions together. I was the first one to get married, so I went from one group to another. And then the divorce happened.

It was culture shock for me. I was sure my life was over; I feared I wouldn't be able to function. I had always had partners with me—first my sisters, then my husband. For the first time in my life I had to make decisions on my own. I was pretty lost.

Many of us experience loss as we age. Children

and grandchildren move away. Retirement can feel like a loss, because we no longer have the work that filled up our days. Friends and relatives die and we may walk the path of the death of a spouse or a divorce.

Being alone and facing challenges is difficult. Today I am part of an ever-growing demographic. Many surveys say that single adults now outnumber married people. Some are single because they have never married, but many others have become single later on in life.

Here are a few things you might expect if you find yourself in that singles demographic.

When it first happens, expect the shock. Singleness can be devastating and shocking. Your spouse is gone; some of your hopes and dreams for the future are also gone. But devastation does not last forever. God has a future for us even if we can't see it right away.

Becoming single before retirement may mean that work actually helps to keep life ordered and at least somewhat normal. Many of our hours are filled and it can help if we focus on the job. Work can feel like the one place in our lives that hasn't changed. After retirement, letting go of work, our daily routines, our colleagues, and even that awful commute may mean that there is more time to have to face being alone, and loneliness can escalate. But this is what I have learned: God is in the aloneness. He is with us no matter where we are.

Life-altering changes can bring grief with them. At times grief can feel as if it's swallowing you alive like a gigantic snake. It squeezes the joy out of your life and makes it hard to breathe. The good news is that Jesus can meet us in our grief.

Divorce, the death of a loved one, and even retirement bring a lot of changes. We've already said that change happens every day of our lives, but these life-altering events come with their own particular brand of change. Life as you knew it is now gone.

When I separated, I didn't seem to fit anywhere. I felt like I had joined the residents of the Island of Misfit Toys. God never saw me like that. He always knew that I fit with Him.

Ordinary life is often sticky, messy, and challenging. Experiencing big changes is even stickier, messier, and more challenging. They can make turmoil spike off the charts into a whole other realm. I often felt stuck, like I couldn't move. I had to force myself to take out the trash, wash and put away the dishes, and take care of the laundry. I determined that disorder and havoc would not consume me. I found that when things were neat and organized around me, it made what was going on inside feel a little less chaotic.

There were so many decisions I had to make on my own. I was in the valley of decisions. In order to make wise ones, I found I needed mentors and friends who could offer counsel. It's okay to ask for help. The Bible says there is much wisdom in many counselors.

We can also expect that there will be a learning curve. One of the most important lessons was not to doubt that God has a plan. His direction for me was never in jeopardy because I no longer had a spouse. My being single didn't shock and surprise God, even if it shocked and surprised me. He always had a plan for my life, and that plan was, and is, to use me for His Kingdom work.

His plan for you is not in jeopardy either regardless of any life changes you may be going through. If you are suddenly single by divorce or the death of your spouse, or if you feel lost because you no longer have a job—whether you've been forced out, unceremoniously downsized, offered "a package," or if you chose to retire after months or years of careful planning—know that God still has a plan for you. Your situation is not a shock or surprise to

God, even if it is to you. He always has had a plan for your life.

From the pages of Scripture we read about a woman named Hagar. We find her story in the book of Genesis. She became the surrogate to provide a son for Abraham. But when Sarah gave birth to her own son, Isaac, Hagar was rejected, cast away, thrown out. She was sent into the wilderness to run alone as a single mom. But she was not alone. She was never out of God's sight. He called to her, and He called her by name.

God calls each of us by name. We have never even for one moment been out of His sight. He has a plan for our lives, and we can count on that.

We are never, ever really single or alone. Jesus is with us every step. We can expect that.

Dear Father, You alone are the Lord. You alone are my rock and my salvation. You know me by name. Thank You for being with me when I feel alone. Changes can come that feel frightening. Help me to trust You through every one of them.

CHAPTER 18

Where Do
Filters Go to Die?

Caring for elderly relatives can be challenging. Sometimes it seems as if they have lost their filters, perhaps because of pain or fear. Older folks can sometimes be demanding or critical. They might freely talk about body functions, which, frankly, is just way too much information and you may feel like you need a hazmat suit to even hear about it.

There might come a time when the parents become the children and the children then have to take on the parental role. My in-laws need much looking after. It's not constant, but they need us a lot. We are caregivers. The roles are now reversed. Our parents lean on us. They need us to run errands, take them to doctor's appointments, and even help with some everyday tasks. They also need assistance with decisions, and some decisions that we've had to make have been important, life-altering, drastic ones for them.

Those decisions have not only been hard for them; they've been grueling for us.

The folks had to move. They could no longer care for the yard or manipulate the steps to the basement. We feared for their safety. It was decided that a ranch-style condominium was the most efficient, safest place for them.

But before they could move, the condo had to be purchased, then cleaned and painted. That was a lot of work but nothing compared to what was on the horizon. After the condo was prepped, we began the arduous task of moving, and as we said, "Movin' ain't easy."

The accumulated stuff from a seventy-year marriage had to be gone through and separated into keep, donate, and trash piles. The Esther Williams–style bathing suit and swim cap were a couple of things I felt should have gone to the trash heap. Nope, they were in the keep pile. Okay, sure, the condo has a community pool, but trying to fathom my mother-in-law donning the swim gear was a stretch. Letting go is very difficult. So both went into the keep box, because it all had to be packed and moved. It was mountains of work.

My husband has two jobs, often working twelve hours in a day, so the lion's share of the move fell on me. The folks are in their late eighties. They could not offer much help.

Tired does not capture the feeling! After each exhausting day, I'd feel like I had the flu. My hands would be cut, burned, and dry from all the cleaning chemicals and hand washings. My feet and knees would be throbbing from kneeling on the floor and climbing ladders and steps. I worked hard. Finally at the end of each day, I'd limp to the car in the darkness, drive home, and then drop into bed. I was too tired to even eat supper some days and yet, get this—I gained two pounds. I guess swelling weighs more than not swelling. Then I'd grab the heating pad, hoping its radiant warmth would help ease my weary muscles, only to do it again the next day.

Finally, we got them moved. Was that the end? Oh, no! Their house had to be sold. The house that they had lived in for decades had to be made ready for sale. There was wallpaper—very old wallpaper. Peeling, ugly, outdated wallpaper. To get their house on the market, the wallpaper had to be removed. All of it!

Family came to help when they could. My younger daughter came as often as she had an opening in her schedule. She is sweet and encouraging. She accompanied me on a cleaning, wallpaper-removal day. The room we had to tackle was the bathroom.

She was crouched on one side of the toilet, and I was on the floor on the other side. Even without wallpaper removal, this configuration smacked of a not fun day! For a while there was only the sound of scraping.

She broke the silence. "You know, Mom?"

I paused, believing she was about to say something kind or wise or deeply spiritual—after all, we were in a bathroom, hovering next to a commode, scraping wallpaper, and that kind of atmosphere promotes deep, profound thinking. I answered, "What?"

"Most mothers take their daughters shopping or out to lunch or even to a spa to get manicures and pedicures! But oh, no—not my mother. We scrub toilets and scrape walls together!"

"It promotes character," was my response. "I don't want you to get spoiled."

The work continued. A couple of days later, my daughter again came to help. I was in one room on a ladder, and she was in another. She yelled, "I'M MARRYING FOR MONEY!"

I answered back, "What?"

"I have decided to marry for money!"

"Okay, why?"

"So I will never, ever, ever—I repeat: never—have to scrape wallpaper off any walls again! I will pay someone else to do this!"

I laughed so hard I almost fell off the stepladder. And worse, there can be a problem at my age when we laugh too hard. Now where's *my* filter going?

The wallpaper was finally removed, but then the entire house had to be completely cleaned and painted. As I cleaned I came across one last thing we had overlooked in the move—a set of false teeth. I did have to wonder which of my in-laws was sitting at the table not being able to chew.

No question, it was grueling work for us, but it was a very hard adjustment for the folks. At times their loss of a filter has been evident. We understand that leaving the place they had called home for many years has been a struggle. They still needed us to hear them as they talked about the difficulty. So we have listened and given them reassurance.

As children we are called to honor our parents. That means no matter how tired or sore we are, we answer respectfully and kindly. We care for our parents.

Jesus modeled it for us when He was dying. Even in His agonizing pain, He saw ahead to the needs of His mother. He provided for her. He made John her caregiver.

God has placed us in families for a reason, and as children we sometimes have to take on a parental role with our aging parents. But no matter the challenges, we must treat them with honor and respect.

There are some things that we may not want to hear when our parents have lost their filters. Some things we don't want to see or experience, especially if we need a hazmat suit to endure them. Regardless, God calls us to honor.

Lord, I know that You have called me to serve. Help me to see my aging loved ones as a gift from You, and give me grace, patience, and the right words to honor them as I honor You. There are times I need to speak and times I need to be silent.

CHAPTER 19

Sticks
and Stones

"Why do you wear them short skirts with them big legs?"

It has become a question that surfaces among us sisters from time to time as a reminder that as people age, they often lose their filters. It was a question aimed at one of us by an aging relative who thought she ought to add her two cents to the short hemline she was viewing.

The phrase has gained infamy with us because of how it was leveled. There wasn't anything to balance it. It was a grand slam in the hurt category. Discouragement and doubt left their marks as those words were uttered. It didn't change the skirt length. It only wounded. It didn't change the size of the legs. It just brought self-consciousness.

There has never been truth to the statement

"Sticks and stones may break my bones, but words will never hurt me." Words can often hurt more and for longer than any kind of physical pain.

But words can also bring boldness and strength. It is those kinds of words that we want to offer. How do we do it?

I was attending a conference in the Nashville area. Thousands had gathered. We arrived at the evening session and only had a few moments to browse the book tables and displays before we entered the main event. I had seen a table with a new version of the Scripture. Did I need another Bible?

I thought about it and told myself that I already had all of the major translations and didn't need another. But it was all I could think about during the message and music. I walked straight to the table as soon as the evening event was over.

I talked for a few moments with the person manning the table, and then pulled out the money to pay for the new Bible. Suddenly from behind, I felt arms around me. I turned, expecting to see Linda. She was attending the conference also, but we hadn't yet seen each other. It wasn't her. It was the woman who had spearheaded the translation project of the Bible I had just purchased. I had never seen her before, but she began to speak. She explained that as

I approached, her spirit had leaped within her. She confessed that she had never experienced anything like it and that she had to tell me that God was going to do mighty things in the future through my sisters and me.

I bowed my head and let her words fall on me like a spring rain onto thirsty ground. I was shaken but felt wrapped up in the arms of the Lord. I was both challenged and comforted at the same time.

She had no idea that it was the first September in decades that I wasn't teaching. She had no idea that our income had taken a hit with my retirement. She had no idea that we four sisters were doing everything we knew to enter the publishing world for a second career. She had no idea that we were walking into uncharted territory. She had no idea how scared I was.

It was then that Linda showed up at the table. The woman looked at Linda and reiterated that she had never experienced anything like that moment when she felt her spirit leap within her. She felt she had to speak into my life.

I cried, laughed, and prayed.

This wasn't just encouragement. It was courage. It was mission.

A few words, a few moments—only a few people would know the impact of her challenge, but I walked away from that encounter seeing life from a different perspective.

Throughout Scripture when angels appear, often their first words are, "Do not be afraid." They come with a message of courage and mission. Yes, there is a job ahead and it will be big, but God will equip. God will be the One to accomplish the task, using us.

I determined to refuse to let the circumstances around me limit my vision and instead discover the path set out before me.

I wrote out her words in the cover of the Bible I bought. I go back to it from time to time as a reminder. Her words have rung true. My life has changed and my ministry has broadened.

But her words are also a reminder to me that I can pour courage into the lives of others. She spoke to me that night, but I speak to people all the time. When I tell the pastor that his message challenged me or let one of the vocal team members know that they opened the door to worship, or when I tell a teacher or a Bible study or small-group leader how much their ministry means, I am planting in them the desire to continue.

We all need to be encouraged. We all need to have courage poured into our lives. It is one of the most powerful ways we can minister to someone's life.

It costs nothing to encourage. You don't need a new wardrobe to go to work encouraging. You don't have to have meetings or learn a strategy to accomplish it. You don't need to advertise or promote or sell anything. There are no deadlines, presentations, or homework. You can encourage anytime, day or night. It is simply a matter of doing it.

"Why do you wear them short skirts with them big legs?" are words that discourage. I think this senior relative thought she had earned the right to speak as bluntly and hurtfully as she wanted. Her words were piercing arrows. They didn't help anything. They just hurt.

But being a senior doesn't give me the right to do that; instead, it should give me a passion to minister. I need to use my station in life to bring courage to those around me.

My encounter at the Bible table in Nashville brought great words of encouragement. It showed me that I want to do the same.

> Hebrews 3:13 says we are to encourage one another daily. Lord, I want to do that. Help me to speak words that are uplifting, encouraging, and inspiring.

CHAPTER 20

Triple X,
the Ultimate Warrior

Grandma, Gramma, Nana, Mimi, Mamaw, Granny...Grandmother by any other name still smells as sweet.

Grandpa, Granddad, Pops, Pop-Pop, Papaw, Papa, or as Linda's husband, Roger, refers to himself, "Triple X, the Ultimate Warrior"... Grandfather by any other name still smells...Oh, never mind. Sorry! It begged to be written. I just had to.

Triple X, the Ultimate Warrior, in the scope of grandparent names, has to take the cake. It sounds like a superhero, doesn't it? But in the realm of "superdom," are grandparents super-heroes? Let's examine some of the qualities of a superhero and see how grandparents stack up.

We all know superheroes have special powers. They see through everything but lead, move faster than a speeding bullet, change into their superhero costumes in the blink of an eye.

Do grandparents have special powers? Can you look at your grandchildren and see that they are struggling? Can you read their body language and facial expressions? Can you discern when they need a hug, a pat on the back, a word of encouragement? Maybe you're not faster than a speeding bullet anymore, but can you stop what you're doing faster than lightning just to listen? In the blink of an eye can you change from being busy in the kitchen or yard to focusing on the one who needs you?

Superheroes can withstand pain. Think about it, Grandparent—so can you. How many times have you watched the princess almost get frozen? But the grandkids want to see it *again*. Have you read the same book over and over and over even though your little darling knows every word on every page? Do you have the grandkids help with chores? With their help, it takes twice as long to do half as much. Then you turn around and hand them money for doing it. You jump like a superhero into the pile of leaves you just raked. Sometimes they want to cook and you are presented with a delicacy they prepared. It looks suspect, but the eager smile on their faces lets you know that whatever it is, you're eating it. It wasn't kryptonite, so you survive—yep, superpower.

Superheroes have great character.

Grandparents can be patient, honest, caring, and kind. We want our grandchildren to see right character, because we care about their character. We pray for them, that they will grow up to be men and women of integrity who know Jesus and become more like Him every day. We care about helping them develop into mighty men and women of God.

Superheroes make an appearance at just the right time.

Grandparenting is the sequel in the rearing of children. We are not center stage. We are in the wings and await the call to enter the scene. We show up when we are needed.

Superheroes are super strong. They can hold huge amounts of weight for extended periods of time. We hold up our children's arms similar to how Aaron and Hur held up Moses's arms in the story in Exodus 17. We can be there beside our children to pray for, encourage, and comfort them and to share much-needed wisdom that comes from years of living and parenting. We can join them in the laughter and tears of raising kids. We can help to hold them up so they can hold up their children.

One night at a Bible study we asked about sixty women an opening question: "Who has had the biggest impact on your spiritual life?"

We expected the answers to be church related—pastors, Sunday school teachers, Bible study leaders. We expected to hear how moms and dads had helped their children grow in their Christian walk. We did get some of those answers. However, we were not expecting to hear what the majority of the women said. The overwhelming number said it was their grandmothers, followed secondly by their grandfathers.

At that point being a grandparent took on new meaning. This wasn't just one of the greatest jobs in the world. It wasn't simply about spoiling our grandkids with candy and little gifts and sleepovers and special moments. This was a calling from God Himself to impact and pray for those who refer to us as grandparents.

As senior adults the generations coming behind us watch our lives. We have to be superheroes, joyfully living lives that allow God's spirit to overflow.

HOWEVER, THIS IS NOT JUST FOR GRANDPARENTS! All of us can be superheroes if we are fully committed to our relationship with Jesus, Bible study, prayer, church involvement, evangelism, discipleship, family, and friends. Those watching us will know and experience that we are 100 percent committed and that nothing can pull us away from that. We live so people see Christ. And that is superhero stuff. Triple X, the Ultimate Warrior, means Xtra love, Xtra time, Xtra prayer.

Lord, I truly want people to see You in my life. Help me to live in a way that makes my family and friends want to know You better.

CHAPTER 21

Running
on Fumes

Running on fumes—have you ever felt like that? In our senior years, we may find that there are some thieves that attempt to steal the fuel right out of our lives. One may actually be the slower schedule after retirement. We love the freedom, but we no longer have the positions. For many years we were front and center not only with our jobs but also with our families. Now the children are grown and gone. If we visit our former place of work, someone else's name is on the door.

We may feel obsolete, almost like we're invisible. We may feel like we've stepped so far into the shadows that we can't be seen any longer. That can steal our fuel, our zest for life.

I understand that feeling. I'm an expert on invisibility, because I grew up feeling invisible.

Even though as a grandparent I can be a superhero, I wasn't part of a superhuman race with superhuman powers. I didn't possess a cloak of invisibility to put on and take off at will. Actually, that would have been fun.

The reason I was invisible? I grew up with Kris, Karen, and Kathie. Think about it. They're triplets and look very much alike. They're an anomaly. Identical triplets are rare. So people stopped, asked them questions, talked with them. I stood on the sidelines. Almost no one ever talked to me.

They sang together. Our dad thought my being their accompanist would be good. Was I along for the performances? Yes. But it actually made me feel like I was pushed even further into the shadows. I was the accompaniment, not the main event. Who even knows the person behind the piano?

As a kid I tried to convince myself that I could be one of them. I often prayed and asked God to make me look like them. God did answer that prayer. He said, "No." Instead He made me who I am.

Was it tough? Yes. Is it still hard sometimes because they get noticed? Yes. But God has used it.

As I grew up, I began to see the unnoticed, those whom the world might have called the nobodies. The hidden ones became the ones who stood out to me. God has given me eyes to see some who feel like the unseen. He has given me a heart to pray for them.

My husband, daughter, and I were having lunch at a local restaurant. Directly across from our booth was a table of eight people. Seven of them were engaged in conversation and having a great time. At the end of the table was an elderly man. No one was speaking to him. No one was laughing with him. The man simply sat and stared. He seemed to be one of the invisible people.

But let's also remember there are two sides to this coin. If we feel invisible, we can take the initiative to start a conversation. We can work to engage others. No one is ever really invisible.

God sees. God never overlooked me as a child or teenager or parent. He will never overlook me as a senior adult. He sees me, and regardless of how I feel, He can draw me out of the shadows into His presence.

Yes, feeling invisible can be one of the gas-guzzlers, but knowing that God sees me can sure help.

There are lots of energy-stealing culprits that can show up in our lives: grief, illness, fear, and others.

For me, another one is depression.

I was fine. I laughed and joked. I was the life of the party. I looked at life through rose-colored glasses and saw the sun peeking through, even on cloudy days.

But then one day I didn't. I didn't see this enemy coming. I wasn't even sure what name to put on it, but without warning the world felt dark, filled with eerie shadows, and even on sunny days the sun didn't seem to be there. Gloom and hopelessness became tangled up in my life. I couldn't peg a reason. There was no traumatic moment. It had simply moved in, taken up residence, and tried to consume my life.

I wasn't running on fumes. I wasn't even running. I was sidelined. I'm still struggling with it today.

Is it medical? Is it emotional? Is it a schedule that demands too much? I'm still trying to figure it all out.

But even in those unanswered questions, I have determined that no enemy is big enough to take me out for the count. I'm fighting back.

Doctors? Sure. Because I'm living in a new reality. It is a darker place than I want to be, but I have to own it. I am banking on the hope that this is a season in my life and that spring is on the way, even if right now the wintry shadows are real. I sometimes face life in a valley.

I want to let you in on something miraculous. Jesus promised to meet us in the valley, and He does.

His Word is big. It's bigger than any feeling of defeat, grief, burnout, fear, or anything else that I can bring to it, so I run to Him every day.

His comfort is real. I carry this to Him. I spend time in His presence in prayer.

I have turned up the volume on my time with Him to drown out the melancholy sounds that can play in my head. That way, His voice plays in my heart.

I wait on Him. Isaiah 40:31 has become my refuge: "But those who hope in the LORD will renew their strength. They will soar on wings like eagles; they will run and not grow weary, they will walk and not be faint."

Running on fumes? Not when I'm in His presence. I'm not running. I'm soaring.

Dear Lord, You know at times I am weary, afraid, or running on fumes. Please remind me that You are the Light of the World and darkness has to leave when there is light. Renew me in Your strength. My hope is in You and not in circumstances.

CHAPTER 22

"How Old Would You Be
if You Didn't Know
How Old You Are?"

Satchel Paige, a major league baseball pitcher, once asked, "How old would you be if you didn't know how old you are?"

It was a family get-together. My husband, John, and I had arrived a few minutes early. One of my granddaughters came running into the room when she saw some of the other family members walking in. Her excitement was evident. She could hardly contain herself as she ran over to inform me, "Your grandma is here!"

MY Grandma? My GRANDMA? Hmm—I am the grandma and both of my grandmothers have been gone for a long, long time. So if one of them were at the door, that would be cause for excitement. I was absolutely sure it was not my grandmother. So who could my little four-year-old granddaughter be referring to?

And then, Kris walked in. Kris! She was the one my granddaughter thought was MY grandma. Kris is exactly six minutes older than me. Have you noticed that kids don't have the age thing down? Our mom was in her eighties when a little guy came up to her and yelled, "Hey, little girl!"

The grandkids try to guess my age. I think it has gone anywhere from six to one hundred. The good news is they always think my husband is older. And of course, I will always cherish the fact that Kris is my grandma.

Grandma? Little girl? Older sister?

If I didn't know how old I was, how old would I be?

Sometimes I feel like I'm still twenty-one— I mean seventy-two...wait. I forget. As we get older, we feel like we're still kids one minute and then the next minute, as we're getting off the couch, it reminds us we're not.

When I was young, I had a very skewed view of age. I thought my grandmother was ancient when she was in her fifties.

Today I have a very skewed view of age. I thought I was just hitting my prime when I was in my fifties.

I'm sure my grandparents' lifestyle had quite a bit to do with their aging process. They had weathered the Depression. It meant hard work and a lot of scrimping and saving. If someone at the table didn't use their paper napkin, Grandma put it right back to be used a second or third time. Grandma sometimes took leftover food off the plates and returned it to the serving dish for a second run.

They were careful about their finances. However, there were at least two times that I know they spent big money that wasn't in the budget.

Grandma was not high society, but she was a member of what she called the "club." I'm not sure what the club was, but she got dressed up for it. The height of fashion at the time was a mink stole, and Grandma wanted one. She hinted enough that our mom and aunts pushed our grandpa to buy her one for Christmas.

That Christmas she was so surprised she almost slid out of her chair. The box crashed to the floor. She jumped up, grabbed the fur, and slung it around her shoulders. She loved it.

You're envisioning a lovely fur so soft and plush your hands could sink right into its luxury. Oh, no. It was three dead minks each clasping their teeth around the backside of the other to create the wrap. And they had faces. You could stare right into their beady, little glass eyes. Their tiny feet dangled. Grandma wore three entire dead animals around her neck.

Grandma and Grandpa were farmers and were used to dead animals for food. I guess it was only a short leap to call them fashion and wear them draped over the shoulders.

But another time that our grandparents spent a good portion of money was to support a missionary. They generously gave.

That missionary was a remarkable woman named Margaret. If you had met her, you might have said that she actually appeared quite unremarkable. When I knew her, she was already old. How old? Old. She was a bit mysterious, with weatherworn skin and gray hair, and she showed up once every five years or so for a short furlough from the mission field in Africa.

When she came home, she told stories and shared slides and short movie clips. One showed a group of children picking up handfuls of ants and shoving them into their mouths. As kids it seemed outrageous to us, and we wondered how anyone could go to such an uncivilized place.

But God had called her to go. God called our grandparents to support her financially and in prayer. How grateful I am that they answered His call, and God used our grandparents to help plant His Word in a faraway place.

Margaret served in Africa for many years, but it eventually came time for her to remain in the States. However, she was one who didn't recognize how old she was. She settled in Florida, in a retirement community, but she didn't retire. She re-tired. She may have had to come home from the mission field in Africa, but her mission of serving the Lord was not over.

The world might have thought she was over-the-hill. She knew she wasn't. In fact, she had the audacity to stare her age right smack in the face and learn a new trick or two. She studied Spanish so she could minister to migrant workers and tell them that Jesus saves. She went to the prisons. She spoke. She taught. She served. She shared Christ wherever she went.

Then, when her health would no longer allow for that, she moved to a retirement home in Ohio, but again, not just to sit back and take her ease. There, she taught a Bible study.

Over the years, how many lives did her life impact? How many people heard the gospel because she followed God's calling to Africa, Florida, Ohio? And our grandparents had a part in that, because they gave.

God doesn't call all of us to a foreign mission field or to learn a new language. Perhaps we have reached an age where the going is hard, but maybe God is calling us to give.

What global impact for the cause of Christ can we have with our finances?

Our grandparents never traveled very far, and they sure never made it to Africa. But their support did, and Margaret would not have been able to go without it.

I have to wonder who in heaven will walk up to Grandma and Grandpa and say, "Thank you. Because you gave, I heard the gospel."

How old would I be if I didn't know how old I am? Young enough to listen to God's calling and old enough to have the wisdom to follow.

> *Heavenly Father, age is a number. Please don't let the number on the calendar define how much I believe You can use me. I want to be a tool in Your hands every day of my life. Lord, what are You calling me to give? What are You calling me to do?*

CHAPTER 23

The Best
of the Oldies

Where were you on February 9, 1964?

Don't remember? I do! It was Sunday night, and we, along with about seventy-four million other Americans, were sitting in the living room glued to a black-and-white TV. The announcement was made that an invasion had taken place on US soil.

The British had landed. It didn't matter to me if they came by land or by sea. They were there. Time stood still. They took the world by storm, and I was swept away.

Growing up in a small farming community, I knew very little of the pop culture. We were not the first kids on the block to see the latest movies or hear the newest songs. We weren't even the last. It simply wasn't on our radar screen.

Old movies made it to our TV. There I met a dreamboat heartthrob named Moondoggie. I was pretty sure I wouldn't have anything if I didn't have him waiting at the altar on my wedding day. Okay, he was a stranger in paradise, but because roses were red, and I could wear blue velvet, with blue suede shoes, under a blue moon, in blue Hawaii, I believed in miracles. It was twilight time for this daydream believer, and I was sure he was my destiny.

But on that Sunday night the first guitar chord was struck, and those four young, long-haired Brits stepped to the mics. They convinced me that they wanted to hold my hand. Suddenly I was smitten by the Beatles.

From that moment on, the world was a different place. The mania consumed me. I chose one, and in my heart of hearts, he was my special angel.

I was no longer over the moon for Moondoggie.

Even before the show opened, the crowd gasped, erupted, screamed, yelled, clapped, swooned, fainted, laughed, or sat with silent tears dripping down their faces, too overcome with emotion to move or make a sound. Pity the other acts that had dared to compete that night with those four shining stars.

Music at our house took on a new dimension. Mom and Dad's old 45s were left in the dust. Pretending to play guitar in front of the mirror, hairbrush microphones, pictures plastered on our walls, and the Top 40 playing every night were now a part of our lives.

I was obsessed with these four young men I didn't know and would never meet. I absolutely truly believed the mesmerizing love I felt would last a lifetime. It didn't.

There is also that kind of devotion in the world of sports. We pledge loyalty to our favorite team, don their colors and garb, and devour a million snacks while cheering and screaming with reckless abandon.

Then there's the Hollywood scene with its superstars, big-screen beauties, and adorable hunks named Moondoggie.

We love to love them.

Why?

Because we were created to love; our hearts were made for worship.

Of course, it's okay to be a fan of music, movies, and sports. God made us to thrill over victory, enjoy great songs, dance with the music, and weep or laugh over inspiring stories.

God created us to worship, but what is it that we are worshipping?

The overarching reason every one of us is here is to worship God.

God created us with a heart that will only be satisfied and fulfilled when we know and love Him.

We have talked a lot about the doing for this season of our lives. We have mentioned serving, praying, witnessing, giving. They are all fulfilling, rewarding, and a blessing. They are things God wants us to do.

However, the greatest of these is love. When we fall head over heels in love with Jesus, it's forever mesmerizing and is the very reason we are here on this planet. His love can consume us.

If the time comes when it is difficult for us to get out of the house to serve, if we have few resources to give, if our windows of opportunity to share are closing, we can still live out our highest calling. That is to bless and worship and love our Lord.

We can enter His gates with thanksgiving and His courts with praise. We can sing and make beautiful music in our hearts.

Our dear mother was quite ill. We knew she wasn't long for this world. Her heart was singing, but she had little strength to speak the words. You've already read that we are a singing family, although the performance aspect is no longer a part of our lives.

But we thought we could be her voice in the ICU. We sang. We sang "Amazing Grace" and "It Is Well with My Soul."

Her words after one of our songs were, "You girls don't sing as good as you used to." We admit that that gift, along with Elvis, has left the building.

God doesn't care if we can carry a tune. Even if our voices are fading, God hears our songs, our hearts, our worship, and our praise to our last breath.

We have the grandest of all purposes. It is to love and worship God. Knowing Him is the reason we were created. He doesn't just want to hold our hand; He wants to capture our hearts forever and someday take us not to a blue heaven, but to His awesome, majestic, eternal heaven.

Dear Lord, worship is for You and You alone. Please give me insight into my life to recognize anything I put before You. I want to know You, fall in love with You, and allow nothing to take Your place.

CHAPTER 24

I Can't;
I'm Not;
I Never Will

I am not, nor will I ever be, a candidate for homemaker of the year. I just can't seem to get this home thing right. I mess up all the time. It's not like I'm new at it—I've been trying for many years.

There's dust around the edges of my carpet next to the baseboard. Why? Because I vacuum the carpet, but I almost never get out the attachments and meticulously tackle the dirt at the base of the wall. You may be wondering why, but I can't really give you an answer. I'm lazy, uncaring, sloppy, messy? All good answers. I schedule vacuuming for right before I have to leave the house so I can tell myself that it will only take a few minutes and then I'm out the door. I do it when I'm frustrated about something, because then I have somewhere for all that emotion to go. That's also when I wash windows.

My husband decided to try a new healthy eating plan. It was purported to be a lot of "detox" with the possible side benefit of a little "weight control." Dave knew he needed both. It meant giving up a number of items, and that included caffeine for the next thirty days. I declined the invitation to join him. If you asked me my favorite drink, it would be coffee. If you asked me my favorite food, it would be coffee. If you asked me my favorite color, it would be coffee. If you asked me my favorite candy, I might tell you chocolate-covered toffee, which, when turned into a contraction, is probably pronounced "c'offee." I wasn't giving up caffeine and joining the detox party.

I was, however, more than happy to prepare the food for Dave. The menu called for protein for breakfast, so I cooked some apple sausage links. Now, here's the promise: This sausage brings almost no fat to the party. What a good thing!

But it also means it brings no fat to the frying pan. I didn't think that one through. Within minutes, the house was filled with smoke and the sausage didn't just lack in the fat department; it lacked in casing, taste, color, appeal, and probably nutrition. It became charcoal. I had cooked the life right out of those already dead links. Everything in the house smelled burnt.

Dave stared at it. It no longer resembled sausage. It didn't smell like sausage. It certainly didn't taste like sausage. However, he ate it. I think he figured charcoal might aid in digestion if the diet proved challenging. He choked it down.

The other day I asked him about a chicken sandwich I had made him and he said, "It's a little dry." I had overcooked a microwavable chicken patty.

Our grandmother could raise, kill, and pluck chickens. She could also spatchcock the chickens, roast the chickens, and carve the chickens to juicy perfection and serve them with mashed potatoes, which she grew, along with made-from-scratch strawberry shortcake. And the strawberries came from her garden. You're thinking I have some culinary acumen because I used the word "spatchcock." I don't. Linda told me what it meant because she used to watch *The Alfred Spatchcock Hour*. Oh, wait, that was *The Alfred Hitchcock Hour*.

Once, I used the wrong cleaning product on my kitchen sink. It cleaned it but also took off the finish. I still wash the wrong colors together, use the wrong products on the floor, and ruin new pots and pans.

I can't grow plants. When I was teaching, kids would bless me with gifts. I got tulips, mums, violets, lilies, a fig tree, and even an air plant. I killed them all softly with my love. Not one plant ever survived coming to my house.

Since I can't sew, cook, clean, grow plants, bake, or any of that stuff, living Proverbs 31 is a challenge for me. One day my daughter came home and said, "Mom, I need to take a cake to school. Can you call Aunt Karen?"

But is that what Proverbs 31 is all about? Do I have to be able to sew or raise flowers or bake bread in order to be a woman of noble character? The answer is no.

Why have we included this confession? Because it's how a lot of us see ourselves. We see the "I can'ts," and they may even become more glaring in our older years. We ask, "Who am I that God could use me?" It is how Moses viewed himself. He asked that same question. God called Moses to speak to Pharaoh, and he told God, "I am slow of speech; please send someone else."

I know I'm never going to be nominated for homemaker of the year, but that doesn't matter, because God has plenty He wants me to do. You see, "Who am I?" is the wrong question. We need to ask God instead, "Who are You?"

We can forget the "I can'ts" and the "I'm nots." God *can*, because He is the great I AM and He will.

When God calls, we just need to say, "Yes."

Almighty God, I really want to say yes to You, but sometimes I get caught up in the "I can'ts" and the "I'm nots." Help me, because You are the great I AM, and if You want me to do something, You will also give me what I need in order to do it. In You all things are possible.

CHAPTER 25

The Runaround

How do you feel about technology? Sometimes it drives me crazy. I hate that things change so fast I can't keep up. About the time I figure out how to use my new phone, it's outdated and I need another one. Medical and insurance information now comes through a portal. It sounds like something from an outer space movie. The learning curve is very steep on many things.

In full disclosure, I don't have trouble with ALL technology. There's some I actually like. I like that I can set up an automatic coffee maker, and it can brew the coffee before I get up. Unless, I stay with my daughter. At her house they installed a new machine. I visited her home but hadn't noticed it the night before. I woke up early. She would not be up for hours and I had no idea how to use her coffee maker. I punched a button that looked like the On button. It told me to empty something. Empty what? I tapped on it, pulled on it. It was built into the cupboard. I couldn't find what it was that needed to be emptied. I studied it for a while, punching every button I could find, but finally admitted defeat. No coffee.

Okay, I could have tea. I like tea. It's a good hot liquid and there's some caffeine. I knew my son-in-law loved tea, so there'd be choices. But what? Most were decaffeinated like hibiscus, organic ginger, or chamomile. I needed caffeine. I kept looking. Then I found some real treats: feng shui and pukka detox.

WHAT?

Come on—it was four in the morning! I was not looking for detoxifying tea. I was pretty sure I didn't want pukka detox. How is that word even pronounced? I was looking for caffeine, not something designed to make my stomach lurch.

Three hours later my daughter walked into the kitchen. I explained that I didn't know how to use her alien spaceship coffee maker. She walked over to the other counter and pointed to the regular coffee maker sitting next to the stove. UGH—that was there the whole time!

So yes, some technology is fine, but there's

a lot that I really don't like. As I said, I hate the "Hello, senior" calls and also getting the calls from Rachel telling me she's sorry, that she needed to adjust her headset and couldn't hear what I was saying, and although it sounds like I'm talking to a real person, it's actually an automated message that says it's my final call and I need to act immediately, even though it is the fifth time that week she's called. I hate getting continual recordings when I need to talk with a real person. And then I truly hate when I type in information on the computer, and somehow it gets messed up. I tried—I really tried to enter the world of online shopping.

For Christmas I decided to buy my grandsons some toys. Cyber Monday came along and I checked the prices. The toys I wanted were on sale for that day. I got pulled into the cyber world by the discount and the free shipping. This would be easy. A few clicks on my computer, while comfortable and warm in my own home, and voilà—the items would appear at my front door.

What could be more convenient than that?

I took the plunge and ordered five toys that I thought the boys would love. After all, buying fun stuff for grandkids is part of the superhero grandparent code.

It was early morning when I placed the order. Signed, sealed, and soon to be delivered. The information said the toys would come within five days. It was just the end of November. I would get those babies by early December and have them wrapped and under the tree with no problem. I woke up in the middle of the night on the fourth day concerned that I had heard nothing—no tracking number, no email confirmation. I went back into my account. The information said the package had been delivered about thirty-six hours after the items were purchased.

What?

I jumped up and went to look on the front porch. No package. It was December and cold, but I walked outside barefoot to get a better perspective, to make sure the package hadn't landed in the bushes. No package. Surely I must have read that information wrong. I checked again. It had definitely been delivered. Then I looked at the address. My package, the one I had paid for, had been delivered to the wrong address. I began to sweat. I felt sick. I called my sisters and asked them to pray. They did.

The next seven days were a nightmare. I had to cancel the first order and reorder, which meant I paid twice. They said I would be re-

~~imbursed for my first order but initially had~~ to pay double for the items and still had no toys. It took days and several phone calls to get my account corrected. It's kind of amazing that when purchasing items online, money comes out of your account immediately. When getting reimbursed, it takes days. Technology is not a two-way street. I had to talk to multiple people from multiple places around the world to finally get it settled. The last time I talked with an account manager she told me I needed to delete my old account and set up a new one.

I said, "Ma'am, I do not need a new account."

"Why not?"

"Because I am never ordering online again."

As we get older technology threatens to swallow us. Sometimes things change faster than we can keep up. Oftentimes what we thought we knew yesterday has become obsolete today, and that can make *us* feel obsolete.

There is a place we can run to when life seems to move faster than we can. That place is to the Lord. The only true constant in life is God and His Word. He is the same yesterday, today, and forever. The Bible is true today, and it will be true tomorrow. We can count on that. What we see is temporary, and it is subject to change, but we can count on God and His Word every time.

Second Corinthians 4:18 says, "So we fix our eyes not on what is seen, but on what is unseen, since what is seen is temporary, but what is unseen is eternal."

If we get overwhelmed with life, we can go straight to Him. We can bring our concerns to the Lord. He never sleeps, will never put us on hold, and He never makes us feel obsolete.

One more thing—the items I bought for my boys? They were toy robots that ran around the floor and made noise. The boys loved them. Ah yes, technology.

> *Oh Lord, You know that I am overwhelmed at times with so many new things, and it often feels that life moves faster than I can keep up. Guide me every step of the way. Even when I'm frustrated with all the new stuff, I always want to reflect You.*

CHAPTER 26

Scarred

I had just finished sharing the gospel with a group of school children, when a young mother stormed to confront me. She was irate that I had the audacity to put children under the "sinners" umbrella. In loud and abrupt terms she let me know that her son was not in that category. She didn't want an explanation or a biblical defense for what I had shared. She wanted to inform me that children do not sin. She delivered her criticism and then fumed away.

I have to wonder how she came to that conclusion. Had she given me the chance, I would have asked. I have worked with children for decades, and the sin nature seems pretty obvious.

To be honest, all it would have taken was for me to take her hand in mine, because I carry the scars to prove that children can sin.

I was born in the day when everything had to be ironed. Sheets, pillowcases, tablecloths, shirts, blouses, and dresses—if you wore it, it probably needed an iron used on it. It was work to press out the wrinkles from almost every piece of cloth that our family used. Mom had four children under the age of three, so she set an entire day aside for ironing. It was what she did on Tuesdays. But sometimes an entire day of the week wasn't enough to accomplish the task, so Dad found an industrial-style iron that she could sit in front of and place the clothing on and guide it as a roller pulled it through. A tablecloth could be steamed in moments and a pillowcase could become perfection with one trip under the roller. It was magical the way wrinkles became memories. Even at three years old, I was so astounded and intrigued by this modern miracle that I wanted to watch every time Mom sat down in front of it.

She had one rule. We were not allowed to come near it. We could play in the same room, but we were not allowed anywhere close to where she was ironing.

The event plays like a movie in my memory. My sisters walked up to Mom's right side and she turned to direct them to another part of the room. I saw my chance. I wanted to see for myself how fast this appliance could swallow up a sock and spit it back out, wrinkle-free. I knew I was disobeying. I didn't care. I wanted to do this. I reached into the basket of clothes, ran to Mom's side, and put the sock in before she had a chance to shoo me away. What I didn't understand as a toddler was that the ironing process required letting go. I didn't. My tiny left hand was devoured as quickly as the sock.

It only took moments, but by the time Mom reacted and set me free, I had third-degree burns on my hand and five surgeries in my future. Skin grafts, plastic surgery, and hundreds of stitches gave me back some use of my hand but left me with enough scars to announce to anyone who saw it that there had been some kind of accident.

The kids in school let me know that it wasn't viewed with sympathy but rather disgust. No one would ever hold my hand during "Red Rover" or other playground games. It was spelled out to me in very clear terms that the scars on my hand were on the same level as leprosy. I was one of the untouchables. I grew up believing that the repulsive scars spoke something loathsome about my whole being. I was certain that no man would ever see past the ugly to find any kind of beauty in me. I could never imagine that a diamond would be slipped over those scars, holding the promise of a lifetime of commitment.

Scars. The truth is, we all have them. Some have disfigured us by what we have done to ourselves. Some have been engraved by what others have done to us. There are tiny scars that blemish and there are gigantic ones that mar. There are spots that heal, but there can be some that still render infection.

I hated that hand. I begged God to take away the scars. They were a constant reminder to me that I had done this to myself. It was a direct act of disobedience on my part as a very small child. I grew up knowing that I was a sinner. The scars were there to prove it.

The moment that I heard the gospel, I responded. I needed forgiveness. The burns were just the tip of the sin iceberg in my life. I could have chosen "sinner" as my first name.

When I received Christ, my life was changed. I knew I was forgiven and on my way to heaven. It was the best news I had ever heard.

But I still carried the scars.

It had become a habit in my life to hide my left hand. After all, why announce the ugliness if I could keep others from seeing it?

But one day I was met with one of those "aha"

moments in the Scripture that changed how I look at my scars. It may sound small and insignificant to some, but it was huge for me. I realized that Jesus has scars on His hands also.

His hands are marred, just like mine. The scars are there because of sin, just like mine. Mine are there because of my disobedience, but His are there because of His obedience. I hated my scars and thought they brought ugliness to my life. What I suddenly realized was my disobedience took Him to the cross so He could bring beauty to my life. I hadn't been forgiven for just a sin. I was also forgiven for being a sinner. He placed His nail-scarred hands over me, and my sin was gone. I saw that all my scars could be a reminder to me that the scars He carries are because of His love for me.

Today when I look at my hand, I don't see the ugly; I see the beauty. My scars bring tears to my eyes but joy to my heart.

Too often we look at our lives and think that our scars disqualify us from being loved or valued or even used. Sometimes the scars become even bigger in our minds as we age and we can't seem to get beyond them. Regrets can become great sorrow. Brokenness can become bitterness. Our selfishness can become self-condemnation. All of these scars can loom so big that we think the ugliness means there is no place for us in the beautiful side of life.

It simply isn't true, because He wants to take it all and use it for His glory and my good. He wants the scars to become stories of triumph and grace. I have since shared the story of my burns repeatedly. My hand has become a wonderful object lesson of God's victory. And just think—it is an object lesson that I always have with me. Yes, I have scars, but His scars, when placed over mine, create a pattern that is nothing short of lovely. I think it must be in the shape of the cross.

Jesus, I know that my sin, shame, and scars put You on the cross. Your nail-scarred hands and feet are because of my sin and Your obedience to the Father. Please use all my scars, both external and the ones that no one sees except You, to remind me to be obedient. Thank You that You can use even my scars to open the door for Your story.

CHAPTER 27

The Life
Sentence

It was Christmas Eve and as our tradition has it, the family was coming to my house for soup and sandwiches after the Communion and Candlelight Service.

It turned out to be a lovely evening. The family gathered around steaming bowls of potato, broccoli, vegetable, spinach, and even pizza soups. Desserts covered one entire table, and the scent of ham and barbecue filled the air. We talked, laughed, sang, had our own candle lighting, and read Scripture. Then the families scurried off to nestle their little ones into bed because sugarplums had already begun dancing in their heads.

Christmas Eve is the most mysterious night of the year and must be savored, relished, and enjoyed, but it should also be ended early, because the most wonderful day of the year is only hours away.

Christmas morning arrived. It meant breakfast and gifts and laughter and tears of joy, and mountains of trash. As I carried out the discarded wrappings, I noticed water covering the garage floor. My suspicion was that on Christmas Eve, half-empty water bottles had been tossed in the trash and the bag had sprung a leak.

The next day there was even more water, so I investigated.

Nope, nothing so commonplace as a torn trash bag; that was not the culprit.

The water heater had died a slow death and was leaking all over the floor.

That meant that my Christmas gift, a new watch, was going back, and my gift suddenly became a new water heater. The mission became to replace it ASAP. That meant getting someone over the Christmas holiday. It also meant the water had to be shut off to the house for about twenty-four hours. Living without running water is not fun. You can't flush toilets, wash your hands, get a drink at the sink, shower, or cook.

After Dave got on the phone and scheduled a professional to replace the water heater, we went to the movies. By the next evening we had a new water heater and water running in the house. It cost hundreds of dollars. Merry Christmas!

Because we had had no water, we had gone to Karen's in the morning to shower, and I was unpacking the small bag that I had brought, when suddenly the room began to swirl. I sat down but realized that my choice was either to lie down or fall down. I stretched out on the bed and closed my eyes. I can't exactly explain the experience, but I felt like I was being pulled into a black hole. The dizziness was swallowing me up. I could think, but I couldn't move. I had no idea what was going on and no way to control it.

I wasn't afraid, but I did think something was seriously wrong and I might be dying. What went through my mind was that it was not going to be good for Dave to lose a water heater and a wife all in one week. I was hoping I wouldn't be as easy to replace as the water heater, but insurance might make me cheaper.

I was stretched out on the bed contemplating what was going on. I couldn't have dialed 911 if my life depended on it, and I thought it might. I couldn't open my eyes. I couldn't call out to Dave. I couldn't speak. Could it be the end? Yes, it comes just that suddenly for some.

Eventually the room stopped swirling. I could open my eyes and then slowly was able to get my balance. Finally, I was able to sit up.

That was good. Dave wasn't going to have to find me dead.

I'm not sure what took place. I suspect it may have been "an undigested bit of beef" or the "fragment of an underdone potato."

Several days later I took down all the Christmas decorations and was trying to vacuum. The vacuum stopped working. There went the Valentine's gift.

Why am I telling you this?

Because everything has a death. Nothing is permanent. Everything will stop working. Everything in my house will eventually turn to dust if given enough time—even me. The edges of my carpet have a head start. Nothing is permanent.

Here's what I would say about the water heater: "It was a good one, because it lasted twenty years." Here's what I would say about the vacuum: "I won't ever buy that model again." I could sum up their lives in one sentence, but my life could also one day be condensed to one sentence.

Dave has conducted hundreds of funerals. He has done services for family, close friends, long-time church members—all people he knows well. He has also done them for people he has never met. He never wants his funeral to be a canned speech that talks about life and death in generic, uncaring phrases. He wants it to be a celebration of the person's life and a challenge to the lives of those in the crowd. There is nothing mundane or ordinary about the way Dave does funerals.

Before the visitation, he gathers the family and asks them to share with him about the person. People start to talk. They usually speak in sound bites, summing up the person's life in one sentence.

"She loved to bake."

"He always had time to listen."

"He taught me how to ride a bike."

"I loved to hear her sing."

"He would give you the shirt off his back."

The sentences are unique to the person. Most of the time, they bring joy, laughter, and even tears. Memories spark memories. What starts as the remembrance of the dead suddenly becomes a celebration of the life.

The family members find themselves speaking

in what we have come to call "life sentences." They are the words spoken in one or two sentences to sum up a life.

However, Dave has had a few funerals where there has been no celebration of the life, because not one person in the gathering had anything good to say. He sat as they complained about, maligned, disparaged, and criticized the dead one.

They spoke sentences, but they were death sentences. The person had lived in such a way that the legacy left behind was a stench in the nostrils of the funeral goers. They couldn't wait for the event to be over. They were there out of duty.

What will be said about us?

Had I really entered that black hole called the grave, what would have been said about me? How would my life have been summed up? What sentences would have been spoken as the family gathered to share my life with the pastor as he got ready to share my story?

Every season of my life needs to have purpose and direction. It needs to count every day. Not for a paycheck or recognition or power but for the Kingdom of God. Every stage of my life needs to matter.

What are the sentences that could be said about your life right now?

If they aren't significant, ask the Lord to

change your direction so your life sentences can include "follower of Jesus Christ."

Dear Lord, I want my life to be all about You. I want to be known as a true follower of Jesus Christ. Please let my life sentence point people to You.

CHAPTER 28

If You're Not Dead,
You're Not Done...
and Even Then

Okay, Linda has made it pretty clear that her culinary skills are null and void. She's the one who claims a mean pot of swill. However, there is one concoction that she is skilled at making completely edible and even digestible. That is granola.

Her husband, Roger, loves it and boasts about it, so her sister-in-law asked for the recipe. Linda was shocked. No one had ever asked for any of her recipes. She copied it and handed it to her. Linda told her that she always quadrupled it to ensure that the granola lasted longer than a week but forgot to mention that the recipe she gave her had already been quadrupled.

Her sister-in-law made four times the amount.

It should have been a red flag when it cost

more to purchase the ingredients than it did to make a house payment. The eight large containers of oats should have been a clue.

The next time Linda was with her, her sister-in-law asked through gritted teeth, "How much was that recipe supposed to make? My husband is getting a tad bit tired of granola since he's had it every morning for breakfast...for weeks."

She had made enough to fill a bathtub—a large one. She had quadrupled the already quadrupled recipe. It had grown exponentially.

Exponential growth...it can happen with food, but it can also happen with ministry.

It began with eight words: "Read your Bible every day for a week."

Yes, only eight words, it was a simple challenge issued by a Sunday school teacher to our fifth-grade class. It's the only thing I remember from Pauline's teaching. She was older, lived in a little town, didn't travel away from home that much. I'm pretty sure she would have said that she had never made much of an impact. But one Sunday morning she uttered those eight words and the lives of three girls were changed.

"Read your Bible every day for a week."

That day she made the challenge of Bible study sound doable. It was bite-size. If she had said to read our Bibles every day for the rest of our lives, it might have looked too big, like eating through a bathtub overflowing with granola.

Kris, Kathie, and I read our Bibles every day that week and the next and the next, and it birthed a lifelong passion for and commitment to reading and studying God's Word.

Then the exponential growth began.

Linda was inspired, as were our two brothers.

And then the multiplication overflowed to our children. Now we use those same words to motivate our grandchildren, and they are reading their Bibles.

Pauline's legacy has lived on in us. The six kids in our family have all become Bible teachers. We have used her words to challenge others to fall in love with God's Word.

Pauline's simple statement that day made an eternal difference.

Though she died a number of years ago, her work isn't done. Her legacy lives on in us and in the next generation and the next. Who knows how far her words will reach?

A short time after that challenge to read the Bible, a sweet little lady named Helen issued an invitation to our family. It was only eight words. "Why don't you come to hear Billy Graham?"

Our family went, and a miracle happened on that Monday evening. Four kids moved from death to eternal life. That simple invitation, those few little words, brought us face-to-face with Jesus. We heard that night that we were sinners, and we asked Jesus to forgive our sins and come into our lives. That decision changed not only us, but our family and our children and our grandchildren. Cousins have been reached; friends have been saved. We've had the privilege of even leading strangers to Christ.

A few words about reading the Bible and an invitation to an event don't appear to be world changing, but they are.

One of these days God will call us home, but our work won't be done until time is done. There are those we've led to Christ who will in turn lead others to the Lord, who will then lead others. People we've mentored or taught or encouraged in the faith will inspire others. It is exponential growth.

We each leave a legacy. If you're reading this, then you're not dead, and if you're not dead, then God has a plan for you today. You have a mission.

We aren't done until God calls us home, and even then our work, our legacy will continue.

Our job is to be ready for the next and the next and the next assignment. Every day is a new start.

Don't quit until you reach the finish line. The prize is waiting on the other side.

Father, my heart's desire is for You to be made known more and more. I want Your fame to increase and mine to decrease. Help me to live out my mission each day so my legacy points people to You.

GET ON YOUR KNEE REPLACEMENTS AND PRAY!

STUDY GUIDE QUESTIONS

Chapter 1: Aging: Drum Roll, Please!

1. What comes to mind when you think about getting old?

2. What are physical changes you associate with growing older?

3. Who are some people that you are familiar with who have refused to take no for an answer?

4. What about their lives inspires you?

Chapter 2: That Foreign Country Called Retirement

1. What is it or what was it that you loved about your job?

2. Was there a downside?

3. When did you begin to think about retirement?

4. What might be some of the advantages to retirement?

5. What are some of the disadvantages?

Chapter 3: Re-tire

1. When have you made a "logical choice" to ignore something and it turned out to be more challenging or difficult than you thought?

2. List any life lessons you learned from that.

3. Do you have skills or expertise that could be used in a different venue?

4. What can you do to re-tire?

Chapter 4: Preparation "H"

1. Think back to your high school years. What were some of the topics of conversation?

2. What do you find yourself discussing today?

3. What is an area in which, if you were called on to serve, you would feel totally unprepared?

4. If it was something you felt like you needed to do, what steps could you take to be prepared?

Chapter 5: Dawn in the Sunset Years

1. What was a defining moment when you were young?

2. How did it change your life?

3. What is God calling you to accomplish today?

4. How might it change your life?

Chapter 6: Get on Your Knee Replacements and Pray

1. How can you be strategic about adding prayer into your schedule?

2. Why is prayer the biggest, greatest, most powerful thing any of us can do?

3. How can you begin a prayer outreach?

Chapter 7: Leave Your Pride at the Door

1. What are some of the emotional challenges we face as we age?

2. Would you consider yourself in the front seat or the back seat of life?

3. What are opportunities for growth in either place?

Chapter 8: Ninety Is the New Forty

1. What are you doing to improve or maintain your health?

2. What about physical movement is hard?

3. Have you had to change addresses?

4. What about that move was challenging?

5. What are some positives about moving?

Chapter 9: Too Busy to Quit

1. List some perks you have found about getting older.

2. What are some areas that feel like disadvantages?

3. What causes people to give up on life?

4. What are some ways to stay motivated?

Chapter 10: No More Dreams to Dream

1. Sitting is the new smoking. What are some ways to add movement to your life?

2. What benefits did your career offer?

3. How have those benefits changed in retirement?

4. What dreams did you have when you were young?

5. What dreams do you have now?

Chapter 11: The Race Is On

1. Have you ever run a marathon?

2. Have you ever participated in a new physical activity?

3. How did you prepare?

4. What spurred you on through it?

5. What was the most difficult part of it? What was the most rewarding?

6. What are some ways you have determined to persevere in life?

7. If you could choose, what would you want to be doing twenty-four hours before you die?

Chapter 12: What's in Your Hand?

1. What is it God wants you to look at through a different lens?

2. What do you have that could be repurposed?

3. What in your life could have a second run?

Chapter 13: Are You Divas?

1. How do people sometimes come across as divas?

2. What motivates that kind of thinking?

3. What really is our calling?

4. How do we live that out?

Chapter 14: When You Hit the Wall and See Stars

1. What walls have you hit in your life?

2. How did you respond?

3. What does God want to use in your life to tell His story?

Chapter 15: An Old Dog Teaching an Old Dog

1. What has God used to teach you a lesson?

2. Maggie the dog taught a lesson about wanting to be near her master. What do you do to stay close to the Master, Jesus?

Chapter 16: A Little North of Middle Age, a Little South of Rigor Mortis

1. Is there something God is calling you to do?

2. Are you willing to get in the game?

3. If not, why not?

Chapter 17: Alone

1. What are some advantages to being single?

2. What are some disadvantages?

3. When you feel most alone, what do you do?

4. What are some circumstances that have come as a shock or a surprise to you?

5. How have you seen God work?

Chapter 18: Where Do Filters Go to Die?

1. How do you handle it when you encounter people who have lost their filters and they say graphic or unkind things?

2. What difficulties do you face in caring for elderly relatives?

3. What blessings do you experience?

4. What are some ways that you can bring honor to your parents?

Chapter 19: Sticks and Stones

1. Think back. What is something hurtful that was spoken to you?

2. What was your response?

3. When has someone spoken a blessing over your life?

4. When have you been able to speak encouragement to someone?

5. How did that help them?

Chapter 20: Triple X, the Ultimate Warrior

1. Who influenced you in your spiritual life?
2. What are you doing to influence others?

Chapter 21: Running on Fumes

1. What do you find to be the gas-guzzlers in your life?
2. Where do you go or what do you do to fill up your tank?
3. How can you help others who may experience burnout, frustration, fear, or defeat?

Chapter 22: "How Old Would You Be if You Didn't Know How Old You Are?"

1. How old would you be if you didn't know how old you are?
2. When have you seen God take a little and increase it?

3. Is there an area where God is asking you to increase your giving?

Chapter 23: The Best of the Oldies

1. What was your favorite song growing up?
2. What singing group impacted your life?
3. Why did you like them?
4. Why are people such fans of sports and Hollywood personalities?
5. We were created to worship, but what is it that you are worshipping?
6. Is there anything that you are putting ahead of God?

Chapter 24: I Can't; I'm Not; I Never Will

1. What are some of your talents?
2. Where do you struggle to succeed?
3. What are areas where you believe that you can't or you are not able?
4. What does God's Word say to show you that you can?

Chapter 25: The Runaround

1. How do you feel about technology?
2. What are some benefits of technology?
3. What do you find most frustrating?
4. Where do you go when you get overwhelmed with life?

Chapter 26: Scarred

1. What circumstances led to your physical scars?
2. What can cause emotional scars?
3. How can our scars keep us from being effective?
4. How have you seen God bring grace and victory into your life?
5. How can you use your story to tell His story?

Chapter 27: The Life Sentence

1. If someone spoke your life sentence today, what would it be?
2. Is this what you would want said about you?

3. If not, what changes can you make today so you can live a different life sentence for tomorrow?

Chapter 28: If You're Not Dead, You're Not Done...and Even Then

1. What was something that seemed small but in reality was life changing?
2. What is the legacy that you are leaving?

About the Authors

The Kandels—Kris, Karen, Kathie, and Linda—are four sisters who write, speak, and teach together. That's pretty miraculous because they grew up sharing a room and one tiny closet but definitely not always sharing. Their mom declared that there were no children alive who fought as much as these sisters, but God works. Of course, today they are still sisters, but they're now also sisters in Christ and best friends. They share a common goal. They write to make a difference. The four have over one hundred years of combined teaching experience but have left those careers to start a second run. The Kandels believe that you can leave a career but never a calling. The call to share Christ continues every single day, so if you're not dead, then you are definitely not done.